Endorsements

I've known Pastor Mark Cowart for over 40 years, long before he was a pastor. I've seen him take a church that was in serious trouble and turn it into a thriving community of believers with multiple campuses.

But Pastor Mark's ministry has reached far beyond his local ministry. He stepped onto the national stage by becoming one of the modern-day "Black Robed Regiment" and speaking out boldly about how Christians must be involved in our government and influence our society. He made front page headlines in the Colorado Springs area when he did this, but he hasn't backed down one bit.

Pastor Mark helped David Barton and me establish the School of Practical Government at Charis Bible College and continues to direct that. He still is a major influence for these students which has produced a number of people running for political office.

Pastor Mark's stand for truth in the secular arena has connected him with some of the greatest Christian leaders of our day from which I have personally benefited. We are involved with other ministers and churches in the Colorado area and are determined to see this state return to its conservative roots. We've already seen good results, and as our influence grows, we expect to export this to other parts of the county to stem the tide of liberalism and ungodliness trying to take over our nation.

Pastor Mark is engaged and making a difference, and this new book, *Army of God Rising*, will stir you up to become part of this end-time army and to defend this nation. If America were to fall, it would not be by murder from without. It would have to come from within by suicide. We are an army of God that is rising up to stop that, and, with your help, America's best days are still ahead.

Andrew Wommack President & Founder
Andrew Wommack Ministries, Inc.
& Charis Bible College

Moments ago, I finished reading Mark Cowart's book, *Army of God Rising,* and I was captivated by this remarkable book that I highly recommend. About midway through the book, I thought of John 2:10, where the master of the feast, in response to Jesus providing such rich wine at the end of a feast, said, *"...Every man at the beginning doth set forth good wine; and when men have well drunk, then that which is worse: but thou hast kept the good wine until now."* This verse came to my mind because the further along I read in this book, I found that the context became richer and richer. Chapter Four is especially confronting, compelling, and challenging in a godly way. This is a book you will be so glad you read!

Rick Renner
Pastor, Bible Teacher, Author, and Broadcaster

Pastor Mark Cowart is what America needs as a pastor right now, a modern-day leader who reminds me of the Black Robe Regiment. Indeed, the remnant is hearing the bugle call to service. The question is, are YOU a part of God's army that will bring His victory to the earth? This is a must-read book. You do not want to miss your battleship.

GENE BAILEY
Author and Host of *Flashpoint*

First Chronicles 12:32 says, *"the sons of Issachar had understanding of the times and knew what Israel should do...."* Pastor Mark Cowart is our modern-day example of Issachar who understands the time and provides insights on how we must proceed. In *Army of God Rising* Pastor Mark exposes the reader to how the Bible coupled with revelation always puts God's people in a place of victory even when the odds are not favorable. If you are planning to be part of this victorious group of warriors called the Church, *Army of God Rising* is a must read!

PASTOR CALVIN JOHNSON
Transformation Project

Besides the Bible, there are a few books that I re-read every year. This is now one of them. In very understandable and clear language backed by Scripture, Pastor Mark Cowart powerfully reminds us that God has a plan that will not be derailed or changed. We are blessed to be living in the time when the ancient battle of good versus evil plays out and sets the stage for eternity. If you have accepted Jesus Christ as your Savior, you have enlisted in God's army. Now is the time to put on your armor and move to the sound of the guns. Read this book to learn how.

Kurt Fuller
Major General US Army (Ret.)

WOW! Esther 4:14 comes to mind when reading this book: *"...for such a time as this!"* Pastor Mark brilliantly outlines and describes how and what God is doing in these precarious but exciting times, where we see that God is raising an army of followers. He's doing the "supernatural" through very "natural" and ordinary people like you and me who are unshakably willing to follow his direction at the speed of obedience.

Vaughn Baker
President of Strategos International

Army of God Rising is divine revelation to warn, awaken, and encourage believers with a strategy and hope to face the future. It will ignite your passion and stir up your spirit, as in Isaiah 60:1-3! You can call him a pastor, I call him a leader, a true warrior called for God's Great Awakening. God raises unique leaders for each season of time. God has positioned Pastor Mark Cowart to be an awakening vessel for our generation. He has been assembling an army of Kingdom-Centered Warriors, men and women of courage who are willing and committed to persevere to the end.

Kamal Saleem
President of Koome Ministries
Author of *The Blood of Lambs: A Former Terrorist's Memoir of Death and Redemption*

Pastor Mark delivers, humanizing our struggle...powerful, thoroughly researched, and professionally written to stir your inner fire! This magnificent work does not generate disagreement but like a lamp provides light to our future direction delivering the vision and road map for the work ahead.

Motivating, Pastor Mark's work guides us out of darkness in preparation for the challenges upon us, imploring us believers not to fall into that "safe place of lukewarm, neither hot nor cold."

Masterful, Pastor Mark provides a road map that our role is to be diligent, purposeful, and passionate in our quest to impact time and share in God's plan for eternity. God's plan is, as the angel appeared and said to Gideon, *"The LORD is with thee, thou mighty man of valor"* (Judges 6:12). Just as in military operations, God had his angel provide Gideon with his intent and plan. Likewise, when conducting military operations, the "Commander's Intent" is the focal point of every mission. Every soldier involved in the mission understands exactly what the commander needs to happen for the plan to be successful. *Army of God Rising* causes me to reflect upon my service in defense of the security of our nation, and Pastor Mark delivers the importance of seeing the vision and mission of God's plan clearly which helped me to know and understand how my personal role of service to God connects with others to accomplish the guidance and intent of God.

I challenge you to be still. Go to that quiet place, and read for your own understanding *Army of God Rising*.

Thought-provoking, in the footsteps of Jesus, Pastor Mark is asking us as Jesus warned the Laodiceans: *"Look! I stand at the door and knock. If you hear my voice and open the door, I will come in, and we will share a meal together as friends"* (Revelation 3:20 NLT). Surely you will re-examine your and our conditions and gain a greater understanding of the importance of the baptism in the Holy Spirit and the significance of being in position to do what God has called you to do in every season.

Sherman L. Fuller
Command Sergeant Major, USA, (Ret.)

ARMY OF GOD RISING

ARMY OF GOD RISING

IGNITING PASSION TO
ENGAGE SOCIETY AND SHIFT CULTURE

MARK COWART

© Copyright 2022–Mark Cowart

Printed in the United States of America. All rights reserved. No portion of this book may be reproduced, stored in a retrieval system, or transmitted in any form or by any means—electronic, mechanical, photocopy, recording, scanning, or other—except for brief quotations in critical reviews or articles, without the prior written permission of the publisher. Unless otherwise marked, Scripture quotations are taken from the King James Version. Scripture quotations marked NKJV are taken from the New King James Version. Copyright © 1982 by Thomas Nelson, Inc. Used by permission. All rights reserved. Scripture quotations marked NLT are taken from the Holy Bible, New Living Translation, copyright 1996, 2004, 2015. Used by permission of Tyndale House Publishers, Wheaton, Illinois 60189. All rights reserved. Scripture quotations marked ASV are taken from the American Standard Version. Scripture quotations marked AMP are taken from the Amplified® Bible, Copyright © 2015 by The Lockman Foundation, La Habra, CA 90631. All rights reserved. Used by permission. Scripture quotations marked NIV are taken from the HOLY BIBLE, NEW INTERNATIONAL VERSION®, Copyright © 1973, 1978, 1984, 2011 International Bible Society. Used by permission of Zondervan. All rights reserved. Scripture quotations marked TLB are taken from The Living Bible; Tyndale House, 1997, © 1971 by Tyndale House Publishers, Inc. Used by permission. All rights reserved.

Published by Harrison House Publishers

Shippensburg, PA 17257

ISBN 13 TP: 978-1-6803-1891-3

ISBN 13 eBook: 978-1-6803-1892-0

For Worldwide Distribution, Printed in the U.S.A.

1 2 3 4 5 6 7 8 / 26 25 24 23 22

Acknowledgments

THE BOOK YOU now hold in your hands is the second edition of *Army of God Rising*. Predominantly, the content has not changed since I received this revelation from the Lord in 2015, with the book being printed in 2016. However, I have watched the Lord confirm the message He gave me in 2015 unfold over and over on a continuing basis. I share those updates in Chapters 4 and 5.

I have been blessed to connect with Harrison House as the publisher, and I'm grateful they have helped me include these additional chapters that show the Head of the Church at work in our behalf and fully commanding His end-time army.

I am sure that never was a people, who had more reason to acknowledge a divine interposition in their affairs, than those of the United States; and I should be pained to believe, that they have forgotten that agency, which was so often manifested during our revolution, or that they failed to consider the omnipotence of that God, who is alone able to protect them.[1]

—George Washington

---

1. Jared Sparks, *The Writings of George Washington* Vol. 10 (Boston: Russell, Shattuck, and Williams; Hilliard, Gray, and Co., 1836), 222–223.

CONTENTS

Foreword *by Lt. General Jerry Boykin* 1

Preface 5

Introduction 11

CHAPTER 1   Times and Seasons 13

CHAPTER 2   The Cry of the Harvest and the
Great Commission 53

CHAPTER 3   Army of God Rising 97

CHAPTER 4   Army Update: The Unfolding of What God
Had Spoken 141

CHAPTER 5   Finishing Well 167

CHAPTER 6   Looking Forward with Expectation 177

Foreword

"Local Church Breaks Law, Preaches Politics" was the headline news in Colorado Springs, Colorado, in October 2012, after Pastor Mark Cowart's dynamic sermon before a packed house (including a significant number of people from the local media) at Church For All Nations. Would you attend a church where the local newspaper called your pastor a lawbreaker? Pastor Mark's sermon was hard-hitting and left nothing unsaid about the responsibility Christians have to live out their faith, including how they vote at the polls. Talking to me before the service, he felt some people might get up and leave due to the content of the sermon as he knew the truth may offend. Being true to his heart, Mark relies on two things that guide his sermons and many other matters in his life: the Word of God and American history.

On January 21, 1776, Reverend John Peter Gabriel Muhlenberg, an Anglican pastor in Woodstock, Virginia, stepped into his pulpit on a frosty Sunday morning and addressed his congregation at a time when inhabitants of the 13 British colonies in North America were struggling with the issue of independence. Many were confused as to the direction their colony (Virginia) and the other 12 should go regarding separation from the crown of England. Was it a Christian thing to do, or would God hold them accountable for what they knew would be an armed revolution that meant bloodshed? Muhlenberg addressed that question in the sermon that morning as he preached from Ecclesiastes 3, *"To everything there is a season."* His final words to his audience were an encouragement to the men to take up arms to resist the tyranny of the forces of the British crown. He exhorted the men to join him in serving in the fight for independence. Muhlenberg led more than 300 men through the American Revolution and reached the rank of major general.

Muhlenberg was one of many pastors throughout the colonies who preached sermons that advocated resistance to the actions and governance of Britain's King George III. After the war for independence, the British assessed that the 13 colonies would still be under British control had it not been for the influence of the Black Robe Regiment within those colonies. The *black robe* term was a reference to the black vestments of the pastors of the period, the men who pastored churches or acted as circuit riders for multiple churches. These bold men were acting on the tenants of their faith by refusing to live under tyranny. They spoke boldly from their pulpits as they encouraged their parishioners to take a stand against the abuses and repression of the British crown.

Pastor Mark has been a man with a mission since that Sunday in 2012. Simply stated, he has been building a spiritual army of Kingdom-minded warriors—men and women who are willing to go when called. Exodus 15:3 clearly states, *"The Lord is a warrior; the Lord is His name"* (NIV). Furthermore, Revelation 19 gives a vivid description of Jesus returning to earth as a warrior leading a mighty army, wearing a blood-stained white robe and riding a white horse with a sword coming from his mouth. His purpose is to destroy the evil enemies of God's Kingdom.

We are called to be warriors as well and to take a stand against evil. In fact, Psalm 94:16 asks a simple question: *"Who will rise up for me against the evildoers? Who will stand up for me against the workers of iniquity?"* (NKJV). This question is posed to God's people, not to nonbelievers. God's exhortation here is for people of faith to stand boldly and fight the evil in the land. The army that Mark is raising up is an army of Christians who have the moral courage to step into battle and the physical courage to fight on even when the prospect of victory seems remote. They know that God has the ultimate say in who emerges victorious, and that will always be His army.

Pastor Mark has a vision of a nation that is awakening from a long slumber. As the world sees an increase in darkness, he sees the glory of the Lord rising upon His people. And if that sounds unlikely to you, then reflect on the times that the Jewish people drifted so far from their God and turned to such sinful behavior. It appeared to many that God was on the verge of destroying them. Yet each time, God raised an army to fight for them and to lead them out of their sinful and miserable state. Moses was called to stand and do battle with the pharaoh in his quest to convince the brutal leader of Egypt to release the Jewish people from slavery. Eventually, Moses had to lead his people into battle against the enemies who stood to oppose them in reaching the Promised Land. Gideon was called to lead the Jews in their struggle against the Midianites and the Amalekites. He raised an army once he knew that God was calling him to this task. That is what I believe Pastor Mark is doing right now, raising an army.

Army of God Rising is a revealing look at the future as Pastor Mark lays out for the reader all that God has shown him. You will be fascinated by it all. But most interestingly, he gives the reader a plan for what we as Christians must do in these latter days. I truly believe you will be encouraged by what Pastor Mark has to share.

—Lt. Gen. Jerry Boykin

Preface

Nothing great in this world has ever been accomplished without passion. Passion is the driving force of life. It is that something that moves you so deeply it makes you laugh or cry. It disturbs your sleep, captivates your thoughts, and captures your heart. It causes you to continually imagine how things could or should be and inspires you to set your sights on the way things must eventually become.

The subject matter of this book has done all of the above for me and much more. There is a passion that burns in my heart. I have discovered what I was born for, what I will live for, and, perhaps most importantly, what I am willing to die for.

Most people want their lives to count for something, and ever since I have been a Christian, I have wanted to make a difference not only in my life but in the lives of my family and many others both now and in eternity.

As I have studied the lives of those who have accomplished great things throughout history, I have discovered common threads woven into their lives and work, whether they were Christians or non-Christians. Accomplishment, success, and failure always leave a trail of clues that reveal the nature of a person.

Not surprisingly, the most predominant clue in the lives of people who have become success stories is that each possessed a deep and overriding passion that drove them to overcome obstacles, barriers, and impossibilities that stood between them and their goals.

Passion lifts a person above the mainstream of life that is locked in mediocrity.

Passion can be likened to the pressure created by fire on the inside of a steam engine that keeps it on track and moving forward. In order to accomplish your goals in life, the pressure inside of you must exceed the pressures of life on the outside of you. Purpose may point you in the right direction, but passion is what will drive you.

Passion creates a fire in your heart that will propel you where you need to be!

If you understand the principles of creating a campfire, then you know this to be true. After all, a fire must be stoked and maintained. It needs fuel. That's why in order to build a fire you need the right materials in the proper proportion. When it comes to fire, never ignore the small things because they can have a big effect. In fact, fire can be a blessing, or it can be a curse. In the right place, the warm and comforting flames can prevent a person from freezing to death and save a life. But an out-of-control fire can ravage property and destroy lives.

Preface

Living in the beautiful state of Colorado, I have witnessed numerous fires in the Rocky Mountains. Over the years, some of these fires so significantly charred and desolated areas that the landscape will require more than 100 years to fully recover.

Yet the fire that particularly stands out in my mind is the one that threatened my own home. I will never forget the afternoon of June 11, 2013. My wife, Linda, and I were in a meeting at the church when someone urgently interrupted to tell us that a fire was raging in Black Forest. That was sobering news since we lived there. Immediately, we both headed to the house!

As I approached Black Forest Road near our home, I could see an incredibly huge plume of ugly black smoke billowing in the sky. Seconds later, I received a call saying our area was under mandatory evacuation. We were given a very short time to gather what valuables and belongings we could and get out!

As long as I live, I will never forget that day and the feeling that washed over me. As we pulled into our neighborhood, the Colorado Springs utility trucks lined the streets to shut off gas lines, and law enforcement officials patrolled the neighborhood alerting people to evacuate.

Linda and I retrieved plastic storage tubs and packed family pictures in them, grabbed a suitcase full of clothes, loaded up the car, and started to drive out of our beautiful neighborhood. With the smoke from the fire surging into the sky less than a mile from our home, we wondered if we would have a house to come back to or if it would be lost in the calamity. The heaviness in my heart and the thoughts that raced through my mind are difficult to convey even now.

Actually, I have seen many fires during the years I have lived in Colorado, and every time I have heard of one erupting, my heart went out to those involved. Still, the local news on television rarely got my full attention. Why? Because the fire wasn't close to our home and would have no immediate impact on my life. This time was different! The fire on June 11, 2013, had my full attention! It was close by, threatening our home, our neighborhood, and all the families who lived nearby.

Shockingly enough, our nation is also under threat of fire. In fact, I cannot help but draw the comparison that there are dangerous fires raging across America even now, intimidating and threatening our very existence. They threaten the place we Americans call home. Unfortunately, there are so many people not even aware of these fires because they don't seem to be close to them or to affect their way of life, or so they think. While people are aware of the horrendous moral shift in our culture, they are too busy doing other things to care or get involved.

Yet if we are to survive as a nation, we must wake up and passionately fight the fires raging out of control. We must stop fighting one another and turn our attention toward the real enemy. It is my prayer that this book will help you discover, locate, and discern the fires threatening our nation and every one of us who call this place home.

Preface

I have always loved America, but in the last several years, I have realized more than ever before how beautiful America is. As a nation, we are not an accident. We have been created by the hand of Almighty God Himself with a very specific purpose, and the closer we align with His purpose, the more peace, prosperity, and protection we will enjoy. It is only because of His blessing that we are able to enjoy life, liberty, and the pursuit of happiness. I do not want to lose our freedom and privileges, and I don't believe that you do either.

The fire that started near our home in June 2013 took nine days to be contained 100 percent. Approximately 14,280 acres were charred. More than 500 homes were destroyed, and two people died in the fire. It was one of the most destructive fires in Colorado's history just recently surpassed in 2021 by the Marshall Fire in Boulder County. But by the grace of God and His great mercy, our home and neighborhood were spared. The fire that headed directly for us amazingly shifted east, then north, and went around us.

On my drive to the church office, there is one particular road where more homes and trees were destroyed than not. Our hearts went out to many families who lost their homes. It was gut-wrenching to see them walk through the ashes and rubble and revisit the memories of what used to be. You could feel the grief as they shared what their properties meant to them on local news. Only the brick and mortar remained. How tragic!

In the same way, America is not just another piece of real estate but our collective land and home. Our Founding

Fathers pledged their lives, their fortunes, and their sacred honor to birth this nation. It is precious in God's sight and ours, but its preservation requires action from us in this hour. You see, God gave Israel a choice land that was "flowing with milk and honey," but there were giants even in the land of promise. The land had to be possessed by God's people, and the giants had to be driven out. Today, there are also giants in our promised land that must be driven out!

The majority of the 12 Jewish spies who slipped in to survey the land God had given to Israel were doubters; 10 of the 12 said it was a good land for sure, but instead of seeing how big their God was, they saw how big the giants were. They needed to see with a new set of eyes, and we also need a new set of eyes to win against the evil in our nation today.

We must do battle to *possess* what is ours, and we must remain vigilant to *keep* what is ours.

Of the 12 spies who went to survey the land, only Joshua and Caleb had a different spirit than the rest. They said, *"We are well able to possess the land."* These must also be our words for America.

With the fire of God in our hearts and passion in our souls, we can take America back, but it requires faith in God—not faith in ourselves. I believe that you have the same spirit Joshua and Caleb had, and it's drawn you to this book. Hear the war cry! Giants are made for killing, and the greater the battle, the greater the glory to God. Driven by passion and empowered with faith in God, let's rise up together and take back what the enemy has stolen.

Introduction

I GENUINELY BELIEVE the very best of times and the very worst of times are ahead. For believers pressing into the Lord and seeking His will, the best is ahead. For unbelievers not seeking the Lord, the worst is ahead. This is why it is so critical that we as believers let our light shine in such a way that the world will see our good works, glorify our Father in Heaven, and be compelled to enter the Kingdom of God.

We are in the midst of a great awakening at this very moment. There will be great moves of the Spirit of God and unprecedented numbers of people coming into the Kingdom of God; but, at the same time, we will witness unprecedented manifestations of darkness and evil. Yet, before this outpouring can fully manifest, we must prepare!

We Americans must realize that we have a tremendous responsibility because *"to whom much is given...much will be required"* (Luke 12:48 NKJV). We must also recognize that America is currently on the most perilous trajectory it has ever encountered as a nation. Even more dangerous is the believer who thinks there is nothing we can do about it because, *"in the last days...evil men and seducers shall wax worse and worse..."* (2 Timothy 3:1,13). The truth is that God has called us as believers to shine as lights in the midst of a crooked and perverse generation:

> Philippians 2:15-16
>
> *That ye may be blameless and harmless, the sons of God, without rebuke, in the midst of a crooked and perverse nation, among whom ye shine as lights in the world; holding forth the Word of life.*

God has an answer to the tide of evil rising in this world, and it is the *Army of God Rising* you will read about on the pages to follow. Even more importantly, God is inviting *you* to be a part of what He is doing in this critical and pivotal hour.

—Mark Cowart

CHAPTER 1

TIMES AND SEASONS

One day the Pharisees and Sadducees came to test Jesus, demanding that he show them a miraculous sign from heaven to prove his authority. He replied, "You know the saying, 'Red sky at night means fair weather tomorrow; red sky in the morning means foul weather all day.' You know how to interpret the weather signs in the sky, but you don't know how to interpret the signs of the times! Only an evil, adulterous generation would demand a miraculous sign, but the only sign I will give them is the sign of the prophet Jonah." Then Jesus left them and went away.

—MATTHEW 16:1-4 NLT

IT IS ABSOLUTELY amazing how the forecasters of today can predict the weather with such accuracy, most of the time. Our culture is addicted to weather reports as we check,

"Will we need an umbrella tomorrow? How about snow boots?" Today's forecasters have many tools that assist them in predicting weather patterns, especially supercomputers and satellites. In Jesus' day, they did it all the old-fashioned way. Even without the sophisticated equipment we have today, people were able to tell if the weather was going to be good or bad by simply using the power of observation and following the trends they recognized.

Using the weather app on my iPhone, I can pull up weather forecasts for almost any place in the world. This is really important for people like me who do a lot of traveling and have friends who live all over the world. When I am planning a visit with them, part of my travel tradition is to open my favorite weather app and check the current and projected forecasts. This information is a huge help in preparing what clothes and accessories to take.

But Jesus has something interesting to say about all this. In Matthew 16 that we just read, Jesus makes a noteworthy observation. In present-day terminology, Jesus points out that modern man can predict the weather, but he cannot discern the times in which he lives. Isn't it amazing how we can predict so many things, and yet, we miss the obvious?

I recall a number of times here in Colorado when I was enjoying a sunny day with mild temperatures when suddenly a weather alert would pop up on my phone showing a winter storm warning. I remember glancing out the window thinking, "It's beautiful out there! I don't see any indication at all of a storm coming!" What did I do? I ignored the warning and paid the price for it. I missed the opportunity to prepare for the storm.

Over time, however, I learned not to ignore those warnings and began making the necessary preparations—regardless of the weather outside at that moment in time. We all know what those preparations entail. It demands things like filling up your vehicle's gas tank and stopping by the grocery store to get food and other necessities. For people who require medicines or special medical equipment, it is especially important to plan ahead.

I remember one particular winter storm warning I didn't take seriously. Because of that mistake, my family ended up stuck in the house for three days. In fact, the entire city was shut down! During these massive snowstorms, personnel on Fort Carson Army base and other law enforcement agencies had to use their emergency vehicles to rescue people stranded because of the amount of snow. It is amazing how much we take for granted simple things such as being able to run to the store at any time to grab whatever we need at that moment. It is only when critical services and supplies are interrupted that we truly understand how important it is to heed the warnings and plan properly.

Apparently, I wasn't the only one that week who didn't heed the warning and learned a lesson. We had another winter storm warning, but this time I thought, *I'm not going to be caught off guard on this one!* So, I hurried to the store to load up on groceries, gas up my vehicle, and do all the other necessary preparations. I even texted my wife asking if she could think of anything else we may need. I didn't want to get caught off guard again and forget some necessary item when the storm hit. To my surprise, there were people everywhere doing the same thing.

When I got into the store and began walking up and down the aisles, I was shocked. The shelves were almost completely empty, and not one flake of snow had fallen yet. It was obvious that a whole lot of us had learned our lesson last time around. Even the evening news covered the run on the grocery stores, showing row after row of empty shelves.

Unfortunately, most of us have short memories, especially when we find ourselves in times of suffering, loss, or tragedy. I realize that missing a few groceries is not a serious issue at all compared to life's tragedies, but there is a greater lesson to be learned from this situation. Most of us have enough food in our houses to last a significant amount of time. What we fail to factor in is one vital bit of information. We assume that our country will run smoothly most of the time. We have electricity for our homes, internet, cell phone signals, gasoline and diesel for our vehicles, stocked grocery stores, civil peace, and more. But have we ever stopped to consider what would happen if our normal everyday lives were seriously interrupted? Would we recognize the signs? Would we be prepared?

Think about what the coronavirus taught us in 2020. Our lives were interrupted in ways none of us could have ever imagined. Travel was restricted or suspended, restaurants closed down, and the list goes on.

"To everything there is a season, a time to every purpose under the heaven" (Ecclesiastes 3:1 NKJV). Reading this verse, we see three critical words that stand out and require attention:

1. There is a season for everything in life.
2. Timing is of the essence.
3. Purpose is attached to seasons and timing.

All three themes are critical to our basic understanding of the ebb and flow of life, and they determine how successful we will be. If you are to be victorious and succeed in life, you need to know what season of your life you are in. If you fail to discern your season or the season our world is in, you run the risk of making huge mistakes.

Prayer is most effective when it is in proper synchronization with your season. Otherwise, your prayers will be ineffectual. Timing is also critical, and, in some situations, timing is everything. If you attempt to accomplish a certain task when the timing is not right, you will encounter trouble. Finally, discerning God's purpose in your life is a key to determining whether you will receive a future reward or face a personal loss and failure.

In the parable of the talents in Matthew 25, we are introduced to the principle of stewardship. Keep in mind that in ancient times, a talent was a unit of value—as in money. The first two servants in the story understood the importance of the season they were in; they were aware of the critical timing of their assignment, and they committed themselves to fulfilling their purpose.

However, the last servant, with only one talent, hid it. His decision to bury his talent meant there would be no return on the money allotted to him. Because he did not invest his money wisely, he was labeled as wicked and lazy and cast into outer darkness where there was weeping and gnashing of teeth. Part of that weeping, I am sure, was because of the lost opportunity that could not be retrieved. (See Matthew 25:14–30.)

A wise person will discern the value of seasons, timing, and purpose. These three issues are interdependent upon one another. They work together somewhat like a threefold cord that is not easily broken (see Ecclesiastes 4:12). However, if you leave one of them out, strength is diminished.

SEASONS

> Everything has a life cycle. There is a time to be born and time to die. And in between birth and death, there are many activities which have their own season too.... The problem comes when we do not accept or we willfully ignore these seasons.
>
> —Henry Cloud[1]

Just as there are important times and seasons in this natural world that we must recognize and comprehend, there are times and seasons in the spiritual realm we must discern to be successful in God's Kingdom. For example, those of us who live in Colorado know that that January is not the time to plant a vegetable or flower garden. It is the wrong time; it is the wrong season. This example confronts us with an important truth that is hard to deny: if you miss your season, you will miss your opportunity. You must respect the laws of nature if you want to obtain certain desired results. You can try to resist and reject the times and seasons, but they always win.

From a biblical perspective, we find ourselves even now positioned in the time and season of what the Bible calls "the last days." But we have a problem! People, especially preachers, have been talking about the last days for so long that it has almost had the effect of the little boy who cried wolf. People don't pay attention anymore when we speak of the last days. They have been saturated with sermons and conversations on the end-times, becoming desensitized and inattentive to the significance of the critical season.

In reality, there's an urgency about our current season, and the alarm has sounded. We the Church must wake up! Let me take you on a quick overview of Bible dispensations so you will gain proper perspective on what the phrase *last days* actually means. In Paul's second letter he writes, *"This know also, that in the last days perilous times shall come"* (2 Timothy 3:1). Our current period in spiritual history has been preceded by many seasons or dispensations from the creation of Adam to Jesus on the cross to our place in the Church today. God has patiently walked with man through these dispensations of time up to this present moment.

In the first few chapters of Genesis, we read how God created the earth in six days and then rested on the seventh day: *"Thus the heavens and the earth were finished, and all the host of them. And on the seventh day God ended his work which he had made; and he rested on the seventh day from all his work which he had made"* (Genesis 2:1-2). The creation of the heavens and the earth, culminating with the creation of man, was a glorious plan conceived in the mind of our Maker.

God's plan would stretch forth from the Garden of Eden into the future for 6,000 years in time. The creation story can be seen as a type and shadow of the ages to come. The past 6,000 years of human history can be compared to the six days of creation. During those thousands of years, the Lord has been dealing with mankind, preparing for the consummation of His eternal purpose.

It was approximately 2,000 years from Adam to Abraham, another 2,000 years from Abraham to the birth of our Lord, and another 2,000 years from Jesus until now. To fully visualize how creation is a type of the "seasons of man," we need to consider 2 Peter 3:8. In Peter's letter, we read that a thousand years is as one day to the Lord, and one day is as a thousand years. We also know from the Book of Genesis that God labored for six days getting creation in order, and then He rested on the seventh day, enjoying the fruits of all His labor. Using Peter's words, we see how six days in God's time can equal 6,000 years. Comparing the past 6,000 years of history with the six days of creation, it's clear that God has never stopped working. He created the world, and, then from the moment Adam fell, God has been redeeming back the world to His original purposes.

For thousands of years, God has been working and preparing for this hour. We are now in the *last of the last days* of the dispensations that paved the way for the season we live in today. According to Scripture, it is in these last days that we will see an unprecedented move of God's Spirit. That is good news!

Perilous Times

Rick and Denise Renner have been dear friends of ours since 1988, when they first ministered at our church. Rick spoke for us in February 2015 on the end times, and it was one of the most powerful messages we have ever heard on the topic.

We put a dry-erase board on the platform that day so the congregation could watch as Rick spent two services teaching on 2 Timothy 3:1. He wrote the verse in Greek, pronounced each Greek word, and concluded with a detailed interpretation and explanation of each word. The people in that meeting began to understand about the end times in a way they had not previously. To quote Rick, he made it clear that Scriptures related to the end times were written "not to scare us but to prepare us." The congregation talked about the message for quite some time. Their hearts and minds had been challenged and opened to see the purposes of God in this end-time season. They were never the same after that time in the Word.

One thing in particular that stood out to me was the Greek word *ésxatos* used for "last days." It means "the last port, final, the ends of the earth, farthest point."

The word describes the final port of a long journey upon the sea. Obviously, the Holy Spirit is specifically and emphatically alerting the Church that we are living in the last days—the final port of our journey. In that letter to Timothy, Paul moves away from writing about the days he and Timothy lived in and begins prophetically writing of an age to come—the last age. Paul describes the last days with such detail that he leaves no doubt about the timeframe he was discussing. Using the Greek terminology, we can say that in the last days—the final port or stop— extremely perilous times will come. As we begin to understand Paul's words, we clearly recognize that we have arrived at that final port. My friend, we are in the last days!

Timothy was living in the beginning of the last days, but you and I are living in the *last of the last days.* Paul warned Timothy that there would be an intense spiritual darkness in the earth that would produce a unique and unprecedented manifestation of evil in mankind, not only among the unsaved but even those in the Church who did not genuinely walk with the Lord.

In fact, the word *perilous* carries the idea of "dangerous, fierce, savage, and hard to bear." These perilous times could ultimately result in reducing the strength of an individual. Obviously, Paul spoke truth. Look around! We are living at a time when a huge divide exists. Sadly, in many cases, the lifestyle of pastors, evangelists, spiritual leaders, and Bible teachers is absolutely no different behind the scenes, and sometimes in plain sight, than that of the unsaved. In Matthew 24:12, Jesus warned that iniquity

Times and Seasons

would increase to such a degree that even among believers hearts would grow hard, and the love of many would wax cold.

In Luke 17:26, Jesus declared, *"Just as it was in the days of Noah, so also it will be in the days of the Son of Man"* (NIV). Genesis 6:5 describes those days of Noah with these words, *"And God saw that the wickedness of man was great in the earth, and that every imagination of the thoughts of his heart was only evil continually."* In fact, the evil of man had reached such an extreme level that God was actually sorry He had created man. In the end, God sent a great flood to wipe out mankind and the evil they perpetuated. Only Noah and his family were saved.

It has long been my conviction that a flood of evil is coming to the earth in this day with proportions so great that the earth has never before seen the like. The seeds of it are present even now. Seeds of wickedness and immorality are being sown everywhere we look and will set up the most unimaginable era of persecution, deception, and delusion the earth has ever encountered.

Christians differ on when the Rapture of the Church will take place, but I am a firm believer in the pre-Tribulation Rapture, meaning the Church will be in Heaven while those who remain on earth suffer through the Tribulation. Yet, right now, we are witnessing the beginning of overwhelming evil in our world that will culminate in great darkness just as Jesus said, just before Jesus returns.

But make no mistake! While the Scriptures tell us that intense darkness will cover our planet, at the same time, the glory of the Lord would rise upon His people! As the darkness gets darker, the light will get brighter. As hell manifests its fury and seemingly wins the day, God will have His day! We will see an invasion of God's glory in the midst of wickedness and rebellion against His plans and purposes.

While hell seems to be having its way, the Lord will surely have His way. *"For, behold, the darkness shall cover the earth, and gross darkness the people: but the Lord shall arise upon thee, and his glory shall be seen upon thee"* (Isaiah 60:2). The same verse in the Living Bible says, *"Darkness as black as night shall cover all the peoples of the earth, but the glory of the Lord will shine from you."*

GOD HAS AN ANSWER!

Even though evil men will get worse and worse in their sinful acts, the people of God will rise up in great power and strength. God has told us this is so! Even now, the Lord has been preparing godly men and women He can trust, and, in His timing, God will release these believers backed by the powers of Heaven to confront the powers of hell. This army of warriors is unknown to the world and to the Body of Christ. Even these mighty individuals summoned to the army of God, very often do not know themselves what great plans God has for them. Nevertheless, they are God's answer to hell's destruction.

Gideon is an Old Testament example of a godly believer who God will raise up in the end times. In Judges 6, we read that because of Israel's evil deeds, God allowed the

Midianites to oppress Israel. During this season of foreign tyranny, the Midianites, the Amalekites, and the children of the east came up against Israel with a plan to destroy them. They destroyed most of their land, their crops, and their work animals and left them helpless and hopeless. Impoverished by their enemies, all of Israel cried out to the Lord. The Lord heard their cry and sent a prophet to deliver a sobering message to them.

God reminded them that He had delivered them from the Egyptians and from their enemies in the wilderness and then finally brought them into the Promised Land. The prophet then reminded them that they were in this situation because they did not obey the voice of the Lord.

During that time, the Lord sent His angel to visit Gideon. It happened on a day that he was threshing wheat by a winepress in order to hide it from the Midianites. The angel appeared and said, *"The Lord is with thee, thou mighty man of valor"* (Judges 6:12). No doubt this took Gideon totally by surprise; he probably looked around to see who the angel was talking to. It could not be him!

Somewhat incredulous, Gideon responded: *"Oh my Lord, if the Lord be with us, why then is all this befallen us? and where be all his miracles which our fathers told us of, saying, Did not the Lord bring us up from Egypt? but now the Lord hath forsaken us, and delivered us into the hands of the Midianites"* (Judges 6:13). That sounds familiar to me. During these days of crisis, I've heard many people throughout the Body of Christ ask the same question: Why is all of this chaos and turmoil happening in our country? Why me?

The angel of the Lord didn't give them a long, drawn-out answer. Judges 6:14 simply says, *"Then the Lord turned to him and said, 'Go with the strength you have, and rescue Israel from the Midianites. I am sending you!"* (NLT).

Gideon struggled with this response thinking surely he was NOT the answer to Israel's problems. He pushed back and told the Lord that He must be wrong. He reminded the Lord (as if the Lord did not already know) that his clan was the weakest in Manasseh, and he was the least in his father's house. Not only that, but the Midianites and Amalekites were a band of terrorists who were of the same spirit and used the same tactics as the terrorists in our times. So, I can just imagine the Lord smiling as He answered Gideon with a simple—yet profound—response: *"...Surely I will be with you, and you shall defeat the Midianites as one man"* (Judges 6:16 NKJV). Now, that's what I call a fixed fight with God tipping the scales. God would so thoroughly empower Gideon that it was as if he fought only one single man! They were all going down!

Still struggling with his own perceived weakness and low self-esteem, Gideon softly said to the Lord, *"If now I have found favor in your eyes, give me a sign that it is really you talking to me"* (see Judges 6:17 NIV). Gideon told the Lord to wait there until he returned with his offering to present to the Lord. Gideon was committed to his relationship with God and did not want to miss this season given to him. After Gideon meticulously prepared the offering, he presented it. The angel of the Lord then touched it, and the fire of God consumed it. This manifestation of God's presence and power strengthened Gideon. In the final scene of this encounter, the Lord reassured him to be at peace and not to fear; He told him that he would not die.

That same night, Gideon built an altar to the Lord and called it *"the Lord Is Peace"* (Judges 6:24 NIV). The time came for Gideon to do as the Lord commanded and tear down the altars of Baal. This act created quite a stir among the people the following day when they saw what had been done. Fear gripped them, and they went throughout the camp trying to find out who had done this deed. Finally, someone said that it was Gideon. They were about to kill Gideon for fear that his act would bring down the wrath of the Midianites.

On that day, Gideon's father stood up in defense of his son and gave him the name Jerubbaal after he tore down the altar of Baal. Jerubbaal means *"let Baal contend"* (Judges 6:32 NIV). I'm not sure what his father was trying to say, but one thing we know for sure, when you start dealing with people's idols, there will be war. Spiritual warfare always takes place around altars, which I will write more about later.

Gideon was what the world would call a complete nobody. Few people knew him, and he offered no real talent or military expertise; but God had visited him and empowered him to deliver his entire nation! The odds for victory were not in Gideon's favor; they were outnumbered 32,000 to 135,000. As if that was not bad enough, in Judges 7, the Lord tells Gideon there were too many men with him, and it could tempt Israel to think it was their own strength that gave them the victory. So the Lord tells Gideon to let the fearful go home (Judges 7:3). I can almost hear Gideon thinking, "Are You serious, Lord?" The real power of this story is found in this one thought: The Lord can save with many, or He can save with just a few, but it is *"not by might nor by power, but by* [His] *Spirit"* (Zechariah 4:6 NIV).

Anyone hesitant, fearful, or timid is absolutely no good for battle and should be sent home. But sending the fearful home took Gideon's forces down to 10,000. Shockingly enough, the Lord told Gideon that was still too many men.

"We need to level the playing field and reduce the army even more!" the Lord said.

"What? Are you kidding me?!" Gideon thought.

Israel was outnumbered almost 14 to 1 after the first reduction. Yet the Lord sent even more troops home. He instructed Gideon to take the men down to the river to get a drink. Men who got down on their knees to drink were sent home because the Lord determined they weren't ready for battle.

A Side Note to Encourage Pastors

Whether Gideon realized it or not, he was better off with fewer men. In the same way, pastors, do not be discouraged when you speak the truth and are left with fewer congregation members. A good friend of mine says it this way, "speak the truth whether it fills the room or empties it." Regardless of the size of your congregation, it never feels good when people leave. But if you are not careful, the departure will cause you to talk to the empty chairs instead of the chairs that have people in them who genuinely love the Lord, love you, and are with you.

Seek the Lord and trust Him, regardless of who comes and who goes. There have been times I was heartbroken when people left the church. Of course, it's easier to say this now looking back, but pastors learn from the demands that press heavily against them. Suffering and rejection are how we learn and grow. We mature in the fire, and we grow spiritually in the storms. Hebrews 5:8 reminds us that we learn by the things we suffer. Suffering gives us the opportunity to develop in humility, gives us opportunities to forgive, and can be the driving force that conforms us into the image of Christ.

On several occasions, I actually rejoiced when some individuals left the church—especially after who they really were and what they had been doing came to light.

Sometimes, the Lord in His grace removes people from our lives because He sees what is really there. Every Christian who follows hard after the Lord will experience this. If you don't let people go, it can hinder the work of the Lord in your life. When the Lord removes people from your life who are competing against the purpose of God, never regret it!

Abraham and Lot had to be separated, but it was a good thing for Abraham. Genesis 13:14 says that after Lot was separated from Abraham, the Lord spoke to Abraham and said, *"All the land you can see you can have."* It is amazing that after some people are divinely removed from your life (whether it be friends, staff, or church members), it will often open the door for the blessing of the Lord to come flooding in.

People do one of two things in your life: they either add and multiply or subtract and divide. It is a law of nature that pruning can bring about new growth. Those who are with you will not leave, and those who are not with you, cannot stay. The only One you should really care about is the Lord. If He is with you, then you are good.

Lean, Mean Fighting Machine

So after God in His wisdom streamlined the army, Gideon had 300 men left to take on an army of 135,000 demon-possessed terrorists. They were ISIS-type warriors who were bloodthirsty and full of the devil, but God was looking for a fight. He was ready to deliver His people and set them free from their afflictions.

ISIS is nothing in the eyes of God, and no one can intimidate Him. If God is not intimidated, none of us should be intimidated. Gideon was His man. God chose an unknown, fearful man to bring deliverance to Israel. Not only that, He reduced their numbers to a ridiculous size.

God had a purpose, and He made it clear to Gideon. An insignificant, outnumbered band of Jews would destroy the mighty armies of Midian, and Israel would never forget where the power and the victory came from. Friend, there are lessons here for us today!

In fact, Paul picked up on this in his letter to the Christians in Corinth: *"God has chosen the weak things of the world to put to shame the things which are mighty; and the base things of the world and the things which are despised God has chosen, and the things which are not, to bring to nothing the things that are, that no flesh should glory in His presence"* (1 Corinthians 1:27-29 NKJV).

The Lord did just as He promised. Gideon's 300 took on the Midianites, as though they were 1 man, and defeated them, all to the glory of God.

The Early Rain and the Latter Rain

So many of what are deemed miracles today in the Body of Christ and what some people call the gifts of the Spirit are counterfeits and cheap imitations. Because of this, Christians are laughed at and given little respect. Why do we settle for artificial manifestations of God's power and glory when we can have the real thing?

Some Christian meetings are nothing but the work of crowd manipulators while others have tapped into the powers of darkness and are producing lying signs and wonders. When the real power of God manifests, you won't need someone with a microphone to tell you that "God is in this place...." You will know it! I am not saying it is wrong for a minister to say that, but when the awesome, manifest presence of God shows up, you won't need anyone to tell you.

In a genuine move of God, the glory of God is released and defeats and destroys our enemies and blesses His loved ones in a warm and supernatural embrace. That is what we seek and long for. Why settle for cheap substitutes when we can experience an authentic unveiling of God's presence and glory?

Psalm 9:1-3

I will praise thee, O Lord, with my whole heart; I will shew forth all thy marvelous works. I will be glad and rejoice in thee: I will sing praise to thy name, O thou most High. When mine enemies are turned back, they shall fall and perish at thy presence.

We must never forget that it is His glory, His presence, that does the work in us and through us; it is not our strength. Why do we boast in what is not ours? Why do we seek the praises of men rather than the presence of God? Paul had it right when he wrote:

1 Corinthians 2:4-5 NKJV

And my speech and my preaching were not with persuasive words of human wisdom, but in demonstration of the Spirit and of power, that your faith should not be in the wisdom of men but in the power of God.

Church services will not defeat the devil, only God's presence will. The church is meaningless without that manifest presence. In the Book of Acts, we see what I believe is the early rain of God's Spirit, and it is mind-boggling!

Sounds of a rushing mighty wind came into a prayer meeting where tongues of fire rested upon people who spoke in other tongues, and the manifest presence of God was so powerful that the locals thought they were drunk. Buildings shook, and people died from telling "little white lies" (see Acts 5:3-10). Politicians who refused to give God the glory were smitten by the angel of the Lord and died instantly, being consumed by worms (see Acts 12:21-23), and the list goes on. Folks, this was just the early rain! Can you imagine what is coming to us in this generation when the latter rain falls? Get ready!

The latter rain was prophesied for our day in Hosea 6:3, Joel 2:23, and Zechariah 10:1 and will culminate in what I believe to be the greatest move planet Earth has ever witnessed. The last remaining unreached people groups on earth will hear the gospel and have the opportunity to be saved. Even now, I believe we are in the very beginning of this great latter rain.

During the early rain we just read about in the Book of Acts, persecution increased against the Church but so did the glory of God! Peter was thrown in prison; and, in answer to an all-night prayer meeting, an angel of the Lord woke him up and led him out of the jail, and huge gates opened supernaturally. Peter came to himself, not knowing if he just had a vision or if this was real. God will always have a counter-offensive to turn back the tide of the enemy's advance when His people walk in obedience.

The Body of Christ has not been called to run and hide in caves waiting for the Lord to come rescue them out of this world. The end-time Church will be a glorious Church that will rise in great power with heavenly authority and with signs and wonders as the norm, bringing in an unprecedented harvest of souls. We need a new set of eyes to see with Heaven's perspective what God wants to do in our generation.

God has equipped His Church with gifts and ministries to empower and equip the saints to bring in this end-time revival.

> Ephesians 4:11–13 NLT
>
> *Now these are the gifts Christ gave to the church: the apostles, the prophets, the evangelists, and the pastors and teachers. Their responsibility is to equip God's people to do His work and build up the church, the body of Christ. This will continue until we all come to such unity in our faith and knowledge of God's Son that we will be mature in the Lord, measuring up to the full and complete standard of Christ.*

Joel spoke of the rain of God's Spirit that would be poured out in the last days. In Acts 2:16, we read that on the day of Pentecost, Peter stood up and said, *"This is what was spoken by the prophet Joel"* (NKJV). This was the early rain, the first rain of the pouring out of God's Spirit on the earth. The rain fell, and the Church was birthed in a great manifestation of power and a massive ingathering of people. However, we know a day is coming soon when we see the early rain and a latter rain combined, coming down all at once in glory and power to accomplish the purposes of God and usher in the end of this age.

The thing that makes a great movie is a great ending. The best screenwriters know how to develop characters, weave the plot to create mystery, and keep you on the edge of your seat until the conclusion makes you say, "Wow!" God is that great screenwriter. The story He has written is filled with the most unusual characters and magnificent plot. Right now, we are living in that mystery before the close of the age.

Prophecy teachers who generate fear and defeat are not speaking the word of the Lord. There is no way God will close out the Church age with a finale of defeat. He is coming for a glorious Church without spot, wrinkle, blemish, or any such thing. Jesus will personally rapture the Church prior to the beginning of the Tribulation, which will be seven years of the worst history of mankind on planet Earth. Jesus said there never has been a time of such trouble and never will be again. But before that day comes, God will cause His rain to fall, and He will reap a glorious final harvest of souls.

> Joel 2:23
>
> *Be glad then, ye children of Zion, and rejoice in the Lord your God: for he hath given you the former rain moderately, and he will cause to come down for you the rain, the former rain, and the latter rain in the first month.*

It is my conviction that we will see everything and more that is recorded in the Book of Acts. The Lord promised that we will see the early rain (what we see in the Book of Acts) combined with the latter rain (what is beginning to pour out right now) all combined at one time in one stunning and spectacular display of His presence.

> James 5:7
>
> *Be patient therefore, brethren, unto the coming of the Lord. Behold, the husbandman waiteth for the precious fruit of the earth, and hath long patience for it, until he receive the early and latter rain.*

HERE BY PERMISSION OF THE CHURCH

Sadly, much of the Church has been lukewarm and sleepy, which is the most dangerous place Christians can be. In other words, lukewarm Christians fit into the church setting, but they are also comfortable in the world. "But doesn't that mean these Christians blend in well in both places?" somebody might ask. No, that is not our assignment! First John 5:19 says, *"We know that we are children of God and that the world around us is under the control of the evil one"* (NLT). The truth is, a weak, timid, lukewarm, hypocritical, ineffective, doubting Church cannot be the source of what God wants to do in this age.

Jesus warned the Laodiceans that He was calling them to make a decision. Think about it; He was on the outside of His Church that He died for, saying, *"Look! I stand at the door and knock. If you hear my voice and open the door, I will come in, and we will share a meal together as friends"* (Revelation 3:20 NLT).

But you must read Revelation 3:16 to properly understand what Jesus was saying. I know we have used this scripture for altar calls for sinners to get saved, but, in actuality, this was Jesus calling His Church, the Body of Christ in Laodicea, to repent or they would lose their place with Him.

Revelation 3:16 is a key to understanding what Jesus is saying, *"Since you are like lukewarm water, neither hot nor cold, I will spit you out of my mouth!"* (NLT). The Greek word used here for *spit* means "vomit." Consider this! You cannot vomit something out of you that has not been in you. This is the picture of a completely backslidden Church! They said, "We are rich, increased with goods, and have need of nothing" (see Rev. 3:17). But really, they were *"wretched and miserable and poor and blind and naked"* (v. 17 NLT). Whose report will you believe? Those in the Church or the One who is Head of the Church? I will believe the report of the Lord, and this means that we need a great revival to shake the Church and bring it to repentance.

If I have ever seen a description of the current state of the Church in America, this would have to be it. We have multimillion dollar budgets, beautiful buildings, TV programs galore, massive printing of Christian materials, and more freedom and liberty than any other people in the history of mankind, yet our nation stands on the very brink of collapse. We have been losing the culture wars. Beyond that, with all our wealth, technology, and ability to communicate, there are still almost 7,000 unreached people groups globally who have yet to even hear the true gospel of Christ. This equates to almost 3 billion people. It has been said that no man has the right to hear the gospel twice until every man, woman, and child has heard it at least once. Where is our passion? Where is our compassion?

We are approaching close to 65 million abortions in this country. Where is the outrage? We make Hitler look like a Sunday school boy. We are calling good evil and evil good. We live in a time of unprecedented attack on the Church by the secular world. Pastors' sermon notes have been subpoenaed by courts to check for hate speech, and pastors are being threatened with jail time and fines for refusing to perform same-sex unions. Christianity has become a joke to most people, and we have allowed our nation to spiral downward into a state of spiritual confusion. This weakened and anemic Church has given rise to the increase in atheism. In fact, shockingly enough, this new generation of atheists has grown up right in front of us and come from within the walls of the church.

With all the ills and problems in the social, moral, political, and financial worlds in America today, there should be signs posted across the nation that say, "HERE BY PERMISSION OF THE CHURCH." Some blame the left, the right, the Democrats, the Republicans, the liberals, and the conservatives; but, to be truthful, the blame must rest squarely upon the Church. Where have we been? What have we been doing? Why hasn't the Church opposed the rising tide of evil, immorality, and injustice? Why have we not stood stalwart as sons of God in the midst of a crooked and perverse nation and allowed the bright light of God's Word to pierce the darkness as we *"shine out among them like beacon lights?"* (Philippians 2:15 TLB).

I used to say that radical Islam was the greatest threat to this nation, but the Lord showed me otherwise. The harsh reality is this: the lukewarm Church is the greatest threat to this nation. Radical Islam would never have gained such momentum and accomplished what it has except the Church fell asleep, hid its light, and lost its salty flavor. This is the very kind of lukewarm Church the apostle Paul described to Timothy. They were a group of people who had a form of godliness (they were having church) but denied the power that could actually transform a life. We don't have enough power operating in the Church world at large today to rescue people from the powers of hell. Only a great outpouring of God's Spirit can revive the Church and change the world. And I believe we are living in the hour when that revival is upon us.

An Understanding of the Times

"And of the children of Issachar, which were men that had understanding of the times, to know what Israel ought to do" (1 Chronicles 12:32). The Laodicean church was ignorant of the times in which they lived, but God is raising up an Issachar generation that understands the times in which they live and have been given wisdom and courage to do what is needed, what is right.

A pilot knows how important it is to obey laws that govern flight. Every time a pilot flies, he must understand the four laws of aerodynamics—lift, weight, thrust, and drag—in order to safely and predictably fly the aircraft. If a pilot is off on his timing, people could potentially die. Pulling up off the runway too soon as well as waiting too long, could cause a crash. These forces are established and fixed, and it is vitally important to respect them. God designed these laws to be a blessing and not a curse. Any good pilot has many factors to consider as he navigates his aircraft. Weather can also have a serious impact on how his aircraft will operate within these fixed laws.

One other very important factor to consider is a pilot's responsibility to establish personal minimums, which is a checklist that a pilot uses to assess everything from the amount of sleep and stress he's incurred to the weather, the condition of the aircraft, and the environment. This simple list can save lives!

So many pilots and their passengers have been killed because the personal minimums were ignored. Weather that is fine for one pilot to fly in, such as clouds and precipitation, may kill another pilot. The fixed laws of aerodynamics did not change, but the time and season of the flight did. The environment and other signs were not taken seriously.

In the same way, there are ominous signs all around us here in America, which for years have been largely ignored. This is a very serious hour in our country. In conjunction with that, we must understand that seasons dictate what you can and cannot do. As in all things in life, timing is critical. Understanding timing within the sphere of a season is essential for those who want be successful and avoid disaster.

Man does not control the seasons or the times allotted within those seasons, but we can—and must—determine how we will live our lives in those times and seasons. There is a conversation between Gandalf and Frodo in Tolkien's book *The Lord of the Rings*, which illustrates my point:

> "I wish it need not have happened in my time," said Frodo.
>
> "So do I," said Gandalf, "and so do all who live to see such a time. But that is not for them to decide. All we have to decide is what to do with the time that is given us."[2]

This is the ultimate truth. When we understand the nature of the time we live in, we must then decide how we live our lives in those times. We understand that there are certain divine laws that govern those times, and we adapt our lives to the laws and will of God. As we become more aware of the true reality of the times we live in, we can learn how to ride the momentum that they create.

Faith is the master key to living in these times. Without faith you cannot please God. Faith enables you to rise above the pressures of life and catch the jet stream of the Spirit of God. Faith will change the times and seasons of your life and put you in the realm of what God has destined for you.

"And He changes the times and the seasons; He removes kings and raises up kings; He gives wisdom to the wise and

knowledge to those who have understanding" (Daniel 2:21 NKJV). God controls the shifts in times and seasons, and He also gives wisdom and knowledge to His people so they will be able to serve Him in those times of opportunity.

Purpose

The late Myles Munroe, who was well known for his books on purpose and potential, once said, "The greatest tragedy in life is not death, but a life without a purpose. When purpose is not known, abuse is inevitable." Understanding your purpose in life is one of the most important—and pivotal—things you will ever discover. Yet I must point out that purpose is discovered—not decided! By that I mean that your heavenly Father designed a life for you that is beyond comprehension, and the beauty of that purpose exceeds your wildest dream.

Those who don't understand the goodness and love of God may think that it is pretty one-sided and unfair for someone else to decide their lives. I've known so many parents who try to decide their children's purpose in life, and it was a miserable failure. Yet once you understand the nature, character, power, and glory of God, that will all change. Everything God designed was created to reveal His glory. But when that purpose is not understood, abuse will occur.

The best illustration I can think of happened when I was about five years old. My dad had bought a new pocketknife, something he carried with him until his dying day. I remember I wanted to see his new knife and do some whittling with it. I did the right thing and asked his permission to use the knife. He told me I could but to be very careful. He showed me how to close the pocketknife carefully so I would not cut myself. I took the knife, found a piece of wood and started whittling. After a while, I got bored and started looking for something else to do.

There was a small pile of lumber on the side of the house. I grabbed a couple of small two-by-fours and found a couple of nails and proceeded to try to nail the two of them together using the side of my dad's new pocketknife as a hammer. After the nail got started, I began to hit it harder at which point the knife's woodgrain-like handles broke off. I thought that I better stop and decided to take the knife back to my dad. When I got back home, I said, "Daddy, did you know your knife was broken?" My dad told me years later that he could not bring himself to whip me because of the way I came right back to him with such an innocent look on my face. Because I did not understand the purpose of that knife, I abused it. There is another tool created for the purpose of putting nails into wood, namely a hammer. Not understanding or disregarding purpose has disastrous results—with knives and with lives.

Anything you possess whose purpose you do not understand will cause you to abuse it whether it is a tool, a motorized vehicle, a weapon, or your life. When it comes to the subject of purpose, the most important thing is for you to understand the purpose for your life, the reason you were created.

Not one human being who has ever lived was created for any other reason than to glorify God. It is the highest honor and purpose of all creation, both in time and eternity, to reveal the glory of God. However, as we fulfill that purpose, we cannot forget that we have an adversary. Satan also has but one purpose which he manifests in three ways: he steals, kills, and destroys. Satan's greatest weapon in achieving that purpose is the power of deception.

The world around us is filled with people who manifest such destructive behavior as a result of satan's deception. Deception is simply causing someone to believe something that is not true as though it were true. A salesman can deceive you into believing that you are getting the best deal there is when, in reality, you are getting ripped off. Many people have been ripped off by false advertising claims on TV.

In these cases, all you lose is your money, but deception in your life is much more serious. You run the risk of missing out on God's great plan for your life and setting yourself on a path of destruction. In the end, you just might jeopardize your eternal destiny.

In matters of life, timing is ever so important. I was once scheduled to fly out from Denver International Airport on an important trip, but because of unexpected delays on the interstate, I missed my flight. I didn't miss it by much, less than 20 minutes; but, the fact is, I missed it. In this case, you can always book another flight, but in the matter of eternity, all hope is gone.

Times and Seasons

I believe America has lost sight of both its purpose and signs of the times. In fact, our nation has been given multiple warning signs that have gone completely unnoticed or largely ignored. The biggest and most significant was September 11, 2001. Never before had we experienced an attack on American soil like what happened on that tragic day. We all sat watching replays of airplanes flying into buildings, trying to wrap our minds around what had happened. It was surreal at times.

It wasn't until I read *The Harbinger* by Jonathan Cahn and watched the DVDs of *The Isaiah 9:10 Judgment* that I recognized that God was dealing with us as a nation, yet we do not have a clue about the seriousness we face.

Rabbi Cahn was given insight by the Lord into a little-known scripture in Isaiah that ultimately became the basis for the teaching he has outlined on the nine harbingers. These were warnings God gave Israel, alerting them to turn back to Him: *"The bricks are fallen down, but we will build with hewn stones: the sycamores are cut down, but we will change them into cedars"* (Isaiah 9:10 NKJV).

Some people think of these warnings as the judgment of God. Actually, it is the mercy and grace of God trying to bring a nation that has drifted so far back into right relationship. God wanted to help them avoid judgment. Israel was a nation that God Himself birthed and formed.

"But now, thus says the Lord, who created you, O Jacob, and He who formed you, O Israel: 'Fear not, for I have redeemed you; I have called you by your name; you are Mine.'" (Isaiah 43:1 NKJV).

Through His covenants with Israel, they became a strong nation like no other, one which God Himself provided for and protected. He made them the head and not the tail and blessed them above all other nations. This blessing, however, came in the form of a covenant, which means there are two sides to the agreement. God basically told them, "If you do this, then I will do this." God's covenants always come with conditions. We do the same millions of times per day in America in the form of contracts, but a covenant is a much stronger tie.

As we move into the New Testament, particularly Matthew 16, we find Jesus addressing the religious leaders of the day. These leaders were classic examples of men who strayed from their purpose. The Pharisees and Sadducees should have been the first people to recognize Jesus as the Messiah; but, instead of receiving Him, they outrightly rejected Him. Even worse, when given a choice by Pilate to set one man free, Jewish leaders chose a murderer named Barabbas over Jesus, the Savior God had sent to them.

Matthew's account of the gospel not only points to the past to explain what happened in Jesus' day, but it also points to the future to answer why our country is in such trouble today. More than one person has asked me, "Why has God allowed our country to get in such a mess?" Here's the real truth of the matter: God did not. We, the people, did.

Let me explain it this way. When you drive by a beautiful home with a nicely manicured lawn, colorful flowers, and stately trees, you know that didn't happen by accident.

Someone conscientiously cared for the property and saw to its upkeep. On the other hand, when you drive by a rundown property with the house paint peeling and a charred lawn overrun with weeds, you know that the owner did not take care of the house or lawn. Is the devil to blame for the rundown property? No. The ones who live on the land are responsible to care for it.

Christians can be really good at blaming the devil for anything and everything. It is so much easier to "fix the blame" instead of taking the time, effort, and discipline to fix the problem. In our country it is so much easier to blame the Democrats, the Republicans, the conservatives, or the liberals, and the list goes on.

The effects of the teaching and reasoning of the religious leaders in the New Testament were described like leaven. They had forgotten all the miraculous things the Lord had done for them. In Matthew 16:13, Jesus asks, *"Who are people saying that I am?"* and it is amazing the number of answers He received. The disciples answered with names like John the Baptist, Elijah, Jeremiah, or another one of the prophets.

God, being all-powerful, all-knowing, and all-present, loves His creation so much that He created each of us with a specific purpose that is a tailor-made plan for each of our lives.

The very essence of God is love. That is His nature. Because of who He is, the plan that He designs for us cannot be improved upon. No one anywhere, anytime, anyplace could outdo God. Even the laws of nature reveal His loving nature.

Just like in creation itself, thousands and thousands of years after the Lord created the heavens and the earth, you will not find Him saying, "You know, I did a pretty good job the first time around in creation, but I have discovered a new and improved version. I am going to take the earth and the solar system and do an overhaul, updating the software that I originally installed." Can you imagine what chaos that would create? It doesn't even make sense. No, God does everything right the first time. He doesn't have to come back later and make things better by reworking the animal and plant kingdoms. He doesn't have to change the solar system, rearrange planets and their orbits, or put the human race back on the planet and then resume all normal operations. That would be absurd!

God gets it right the first time! He got you right the first time! Although you and I have sinned and made horrible mistakes, the most important thing is to get our lives back in sync with God and move in harmony with Him. That is what makes life grand! There is always another chance. God makes it so!

Far too many Christians do not discern the times and seasons that they are in. They do not discern the place they are in. Where you are is important. It is true that God made places before He made man. He was in the Garden of Eden, a perfect place. But through the subtlety of satan, man was driven out of the perfect place God had prepared for him.

Times and Seasons

Some have jokingly said that Eve ate Adam out of house and home, but there is more truth to that than most people realize. The Bible says that Eve was deceived, and Adam was not. People often blame the woman for taking the fruit, but Adam could have stopped it! He knew better.

In the marriage relationship, ladies, be careful not to persuade your husband to get out of the will of God. You have such power with your husband. You are to be his "completer not his competer." Through the years, I have watched so many people come on staff and through carelessness not discern their time and season of preparation. They leave in the wrong way, they leave prematurely, or, in some cases, they disqualify themselves, and I am left with no choice but to remove them. Sometimes it creates a delay in God's plans for their lives, and sometimes, they lose their place with God entirely.

"'Only an evil, adulterous generation would demand a miraculous sign, but the only sign I will give them is the sign of the prophet Jonah.' Then Jesus left them and went away" (Matthew 16:4 NLT). Why would Jesus call that generation an "evil, adulterous generation" for merely wanting to see a sign? The answer is quite simple. The Pharisees should have been the first to recognize Jesus because of their knowledge of the Scriptures. In New Testament times, every Jewish male was required to memorize the Pentateuch. Pharisees had to memorize the entire Old Testament. Think about it. All the prophecies regarding the coming of Messiah in the Old Testament pointed to His coming, and they missed their opportunity!

The Lord has a covenant with Israel, which is likened to a marriage. In Ephesians, Paul compared the marriage between a man and a woman as a type and shadow of the new birth. This is the mystery of the Church and God's purposes for His people. So, then, the Pharisees were like an unfaithful spouse trying to cover the sin of adultery. They were asking for a sign while, right before their very eyes, Jesus was performing signs and wonders. Because of that, Jesus said the only sign they would get was that of the prophet Jonah in the belly of the whale for three days, symbolizing Jesus' death, burial, and resurrection.

Those religious leaders missed their season and forfeited the purposes God had designed for their lives. Let us not miss our times and season. Let us be spiritually aware of the days in which we are living and fulfill the destiny designed for us. There is a season. There is timing for that season, and there is a purpose for us to fulfill in the season and the times we live. Never forget, faith is the key that enables us to journey through those seasons and times that are in the Father's hands.

Faith is the master key that makes it all work together for the glory of God.

Notes

1. Henry Cloud (@DrHenryCloud), "Everything has a life cycle," Facebook, June 23, 2015, https://m.facebook.com/DrHenryCloud/posts/hey-guys-life-is-composed-of-cycles-and-seasons-nothing-lasts-forever-life-cycle/10153447387269571/.

2. J. R. R. *Tolkien, The Lord of the Rings: One Volume* (Boston, MA: Houghton Mifflin Harcourt, 2012).

CHAPTER 2

THE CRY OF THE HARVEST AND THE GREAT COMMISSION

ONE THING I especially love about the gospel is the absolute simplicity of it. In fact, the gospel is so simple we need help to misunderstand it. Unfortunately, we have had a lot of help misunderstanding the simple gospel.

> Mark 7:8-9,13
>
> *For laying aside the commandment of God, ye hold the tradition of men, as the washing of pots and cups: and many other such like things ye do. And he said unto them, Full well ye reject the commandment of God, that ye may keep your own tradition....Making the word of God*

of none effect through your tradition, which ye have delivered: and many such like things do ye.

Jesus cut to the very core of the religious system of His day with these words. At the heart of the matter, the Pharisees put more emphasis on external works than on the condition of the heart. Tradition can be such a good thing, but it can also be an evil thing. In too many cases, tradition is the religion of the dead rather than the living. In this case, Jesus warned the Pharisees that their tradition was making the Word of God of no effect. Other translations of verse 13 say that tradition will nullify, cancel, void, or invalidate God's Word.

Tradition cannot save you, heal you, or deliver you, but the Word of God can. There is no other way that the Lord can lift His people out of their lost and tragic lives other than through His Word. *"He sent His word and healed them, and delivered them from their destructions"* (Psalm 107:20 NKJV). The living Word always trumps dead traditions.

When we as Christians, as individuals, or as a nation reject the Word of God, horrible things begin to happen. The battles that rage over religious freedom in America are all about one thing: silencing the Body of Christ. Satan will *never* accomplish his objectives in the lives of individuals or in collective society as long as Christians declare the Word of God and live according to its words.

It is not our creative, inspirational sermons that change lives or create change; it is the living Word of God, activated by a faith that is God's gift to His people.

If you have ever asked yourself how our nation could veer so far off course and so distant from the Christian faith of our spiritual fathers and founding fathers, the apostle Paul answers that question: *"But I fear, lest by any means, as the serpent beguiled Eve through his subtilty, so your minds should be corrupted from the simplicity that is in Christ"* (2 Corinthians 11:3).

Paul compares the seductive subtleties that took place in the garden to what was happening in Corinth. The Greek word for *subtilty* actually means "to present a false wisdom and engage in a malicious craftiness." This devilish use of perverted and false wisdom seduces, deceives, and corrupts the mind so that the object of the attack is led away in chains from the simplicity of the gospel. Sin is not always just some out-of-control deed acted out by some crazed individual on a rampage. At times, it dresses itself up with sophisticated words and classy apparel. The enticement that happened to Eve in the Garden of Eden was not only satanic in its source, it was very appealing. But it was also in direct opposition to God's stated commands.

This same battle continues in our day as we seek to substitute our own laws for the laws of God. Instead of submitting to the law of God, we create our own laws that are more suited to our desires. But in doing so, we position ourselves above God and His Word, which is exactly what lucifer did in the garden.

I was studying one afternoon, and, for some reason, I remembered a pastor who my wife and I had met back in 1988. As I thought more about him, I began wondering how and what he was doing.

We first met this pastor on our first trip to Israel that was a completely awesome experience. Our group was large and included six buses total. Each bus had a tour guide certified by the state of Israel who answered every single question we asked with such depth. Each bus also had a captain who led us in prayer and kept things moving along. These were typically pastors who talked as we drove between sights. This pastor was one of those guides.

As I recalled these trip details while taking a break from my studies, I decided to look up this pastor on the internet just to see if I could find out how he and his church were doing. I was shocked to see the results of my search. In years past, I had seen him every once in a while on Christian TV. He would either be releasing a new book or hosting a show with very well-known ministers. It appeared he was doing extremely well during those times, but something had gone terribly wrong. His life had spun completely out of control. There were moral failures, divorces, bankruptcy, multiple arrests, and criminal charges. There was another article about a teenage girl who had called the police after she fled out of his house, having become uncomfortable with how he was interacting with her.

Finally, I ended up on a page with a quote by the pastor saying he was a follower of Jesus and a student of the teachings of Buddha and Maharishi Yogi. On top of it all, he had started a new church where there were no rules, just religion.

How can someone go from being a respected and young, budding pastor to such a confused spiritual mess? Well, it's simple. Whenever we allow ourselves to be seduced and beguiled by the craftiness of our enemy, there is no telling where we will end up. In the garden, the enemy endeavored to put doubt into Eve's mind concerning the Word of God with this one question: *"Did God really say...?"* This same question continues to cause confusion in the minds of God's people today. In fact, this is the same battle raging in our culture today. Political correctness actually started in the Garden of Eden, and it sounds like this:

- Did God really say that marriage is just between a man and a woman?
- Is abortion that big of a deal?
- Is there only one way to God?
- Does it really matter how I live my life?

It is difficult to grasp that Adam and Eve, who were living in a perfect environment and created in absolute perfection, could be seduced into disobeying the Lord. They didn't have a 30-year mortgage that they were behind on. Eve didn't grow up with an abusive father. She wasn't molested by a family member. Adam didn't have an abusive father or an offensive mother. Yet, satan was able to deceive them into committing high treason against God, thus plunging all of humanity into death and destruction.

This resulted in untold millions paying the price for that single act of rebellion.

Leonard Ravenhill, whose great passion was prayer and revival, spoke clearly on the issue of the shifting terminology that exists in the Church today: "We're living in an unprecedented day (when) evil is no longer evil. We've changed the terminology—iniquity is now infirmity; wickedness is now weakness; devilry is now deficiency."

Forgotten Foundations and Rejected Knowledge

A building is no better than its foundation. Thomas à Kempis put it this way: "The loftier the building, the deeper the foundation must be." Though they are not seen, foundations are critical to the support and security of any superstructure. Foundations are below the surface and unseen, yet they hold up everything that is above the surface and seen.

Several times in Scripture, the people of God are compared to God's house or His building. Paul told the Corinthians he was a wise master builder because he was careful how he built. He knew the importance of the foundation as well as the significance of using the right materials for building the structure on the foundation.

God's Word tells us if the biblical foundations are destroyed, there will be trouble in the Church: *"If the foundations be destroyed, what can the righteous do?"* (Psalm 11:3).

We are living in an unprecedented time in our nation. We are watching before our very eyes the departure from sound biblical doctrine and faith across America. In this departure, there is one truth we cannot ignore—the fact that solid biblical foundations were not fully established in the Church. We have kids who were raised in Christian homes who eventually leave for college and sit under atheistic humanist college professors who fill their minds with evolution and cultural relativism. Our children have not been adequately trained to defend their faith in a logical, rational, scriptural way.

The Bible tells us in Hosea 4:6 that God's people—not the devil's crowd—are *"destroyed for lack of knowledge."* Usually, we stop right there and don't finish reading the rest of the verse: *"Because thou hast rejected knowledge, I will also reject thee, that thou shalt be no priest to me: seeing thou hast forgotten the law of thy God, I will also forget thy children."*

It wasn't that the knowledge was not available—it was rejected. Both the priests and the people were at fault. They chose to reject God's knowledge and did not pass that knowledge down to the next generation.

This is America right now! We have and are willfully rejecting not only the knowledge of God but also the acknowledgment of God, and the consequences are absolutely devastating.

Israel encountered a similar problem and consequence. Since Israel rejected knowledge and had forgotten the Word of God, the consequence was that for a time God looked away from their children.

As we as parents get older, we concern ourselves more with what we will leave our children which leads us to ponder what is more important—what we leave FOR our children or what we leave IN our children? In reality, we are always just one generation away from a totally godless society. If we fail to pass on the knowledge of God to this generation, we will have failed regardless of how much "success" we accumulate and what level of inheritance we leave our children. America cannot claim ignorance of God's Word. It has been preached and proclaimed in every corner of our country. What we must assume responsibility for is that God's Word is being rejected, fought, resisted, and mocked by a humanistic society that has chosen to go its own way. This is all happening on our watch and by permission of the Church, the Body of Christ.

Some of the more well-known atheists who comment today are not merely saying there is no God, they are spewing hate toward Him. It would be more appropriate to call them *anti-theists* than *a-theists*. They are God haters inspired by hell. The deceased Christopher Hitchens, one of the more well-known atheists of our time, wrote a book called *God Is Not Great*. To illustrate my point, here is the publisher's description of the book, which exemplifies Hitchens's distaste for God and the Church.

> *God Is Not Great* is the ultimate case against religion. In a series of acute readings of the major religious texts, Christopher Hitchens demonstrates the ways in which religion is man-made, dangerously sexually repressive and distorts the very origins of the cosmos. Above all, Hitchens argues that the concept of

an omniscient God has profoundly damaged humanity, and proposes that the world might be a great deal better off without "him."[1]

What is the Bible's response? *"Now the Spirit speaketh expressly, that in the latter times some shall depart from the faith, giving heed to seducing spirits, and doctrines of devils"* (1 Timothy 4:1).

There has been a departure from the true faith in the Church today, and much of what is called faith is merely mental assent. Mental assent looks so much like faith that the unsuspecting will accept it as faith. Influential 20th-century Bible scholar, preacher, and author, E. W. Kenyon described the dangers of mental assent with these words:

> Mental assent is one of the most dangerous of the enemies of a life of faith. It looks and sounds so religious. It will go so far as to say, "I believe in the verbal inspiration of the Bible. I am contending for the faith once delivered to the saints." Yet, they dare not act on the Word; they do not give it its place, they merely talk about its integrity. The mental assenter is in the gravest of danger. He is where God cannot reach him; but where Satan can enter into his inner counsel.[2]

Mental assent acknowledges the Bible as the Word of God and agrees it is true, but there is no power because there is no faith. There are many people who intellectually accept that God exists and that the Bible is the Word of God. However, intellectual acknowledgment cannot be confused with faith. Mental assent is soulish, and faith is of the spirit. One can mentally assent to these truths when life is grand, but when the crisis of life comes, there is no power to deal with adversity. This is why we have produced so many Christian atheists in the Church. They essentially live a life that denies the existence of God. In the Old Testament, there was an entire generation that went without seeing the power of God, and they were eventually led off into bondage and captivity.

Hope says, "I will have it one day," but true Bible faith says, "I have it now!" Faith is not a mental force but a spiritual force of the recreated human spirit. If you are wondering if you have faith right now, then you don't. Let me explain it this way. Fear is not merely a mental force but a spiritual force, and you never have to guess if you are in fear or not. You know that you know when you are in faith. Fear in strong enough doses can trigger a heart attack, but faith in strong enough doses can trigger a spiritual victory. There is never any doubt if you are walking in faith when it is genuine Bible faith.

Faith is not hope, and hope is not faith, but they are essential to each other. The Amplified Bible, Classic Edition does the best job of describing what genuine Bible faith is in Hebrews 11:1, *"Now faith is the assurance (the confirmation, the title deed) of the things [we] hope for, being the proof of things [we] do not see and the conviction of their reality [faith perceiving as real fact what is not revealed to the senses]."*

Faith is one of the wells we must re-dig in our generation if we are to survive. The enemy has seduced the Church into accepting a spirit of religion instead of a spirit of faith. There is a demon spirit operating under the guise of religion who attempts to substitute good works and activities for the life and power of God. This is what causes so many believers to fight the devil when what the Bible tells us to do is to fight the good fight of faith. Never fight the devil! In Christ, the devil is a defeated foe!

What does that mean? It means that the mental arena is where you will fight the fight of faith. When you are attacked with cares, anxieties, burdens, distractions, or any other problem, subdue and harness your soul (mind, will, and emotions) through the Word of God.

In Luke 21:19, Jesus said, *"By your patience possess your souls"* (NKJV). If you do this, your faith will live big within you.

RECOVERING THE FORGOTTEN FOUNDATIONS

There are six foundational doctrines found in Hebrews 6:1-3 that are essential in developing a strong Christian life. The absence of these spiritual foundations leads to the complete demise of a person's spiritual life.

> *Therefore leaving the principles of the doctrine of Christ, let us go on unto perfection; not laying again the foundation of repentance from dead*

> *works, and faith toward God, of the doctrine of baptisms, and of laying on of hands, and of resurrection of the dead, and of eternal judgment. And this will we do, if God permit.*

Unfortunately, most Christians are not aware that these foundational doctrines even exist. It is amazing and sad that Christians can read the Bible and totally miss the significance of what they are reading. The author of Hebrews urges the Church to move on past these elementary and foundational truths. However, no Christian can truly progress until these principal foundations have been laid. (I taught an entire series on this topic titled *Foundations of the Christian Faith* available at churchforallnations.com.) This is basic training for all believers.

It is dangerous to even try to move on in the life of faith without the groundwork of fundamental truths establishing your walk with God. A firm foundation is critical and allows you to stand strong and unshakable when the storms of life begin to blow.

I've had firsthand experience dealing with foundations in our previous church building. Let me tell you, not laying a proper foundation will eventually come at great cost! In our case, city inspectors notified me one day that they were condemning our building. They gave us 5 days to vacate the building and 90 days to have it torn down. I was stunned. How could this happen?

We had a 17,000-square-foot sanctuary and a 20,000-square-foot office building where we housed our children's church and main offices. It would cost a great deal of money to tear down the building and haul off the materials. On top of that, we would face the cost of major renovations having to fit into our smaller facilities.

The problem was created by the original builder. I was totally unaware that he had a reputation for taking shortcuts. We had expansive soil in our part of town that required more time and money to properly lay the foundation. This person was known for not wanting to spend extra money to ensure that it was done right. So 25 years later, we were paying the price for a building that did not have the proper foundations. A firm foundation is important for buildings and for Christians, so let's always make sure they are properly laid.

Repentance from dead works is the first of the six foundational truths; although, we will primarily consider only two of the foundations in the context of this book. The writer of Hebrews is making it clear that the first footer of the foundation must be a complete and total change of heart concerning one's decision to follow the Lord. True repentance requires a quality decision from which there is no retreat, no matter the adversity or obstacle. Dead works are the work of our hands. In Proverbs 14:12 and 16:25, the Word tells us that *"there is a way that seems right to a man, but its end is the way of death"* (NKJV). In other words "dead works" are those actions that lead straight to the place of death because they are works of self-righteousness and not the righteousness of God that is in Christ Jesus. Just because we do good things doesn't mean that they have proceeded from God. In Matthew 7:21-23, the Lord tells us that many, not just a few, would say to Him on judgment day that they prophesied, cast out devils, and performed many miracles in His Name, yet He told them to depart from Him. Those are all "good things" that were performed but apparently dead works because of the ungodly lives of those individuals. A religious spirit is a demon that will draw you away from the life of Christ and seduce you into substituting good works for the life of God that can only be found in Christ. Acts 17:28 says, *"For in Him we live and move and have our being."* We are human *beings* not human *doings*. Dead works hinder and keep the life of God from flowing through us. It means that we are not flowing in the life of God but in our own strength. The Scripture says that the arm of flesh will always fail, which ultimately translates in the works of the flesh rather than the fruit of the Spirit. As you can see, this first foundational doctrine is the most important, or we could spend our lives thinking we are serving God, when, in reality, we are functioning in dead works.

Howard Pittman was a bi-vocational pastor who was pronounced clinically dead in 1979 after one of his primary arteries ruptured. After an incredibly powerful encounter with the Lord and a tour of the spirit realm where the Lord showed him the hierarchy of demon powers, he was given a second chance. Thankfully the Lord spared his life! His story is riveting, and I had the opportunity to record an interview with him a few years before he died where he shared his testimony. In that interview, he told how while he was dead, he saw Jesus who had stern words for him: "Your life is an abomination to Me. You have served Me in a pharisaical fashion of dead works. You did all of these things for yourself." The most sobering part of his testimony is the fact that he was a model pastor, husband, and father!

Faith is the second of the six foundational truths, and it is the opposite of dead works. The person of faith puts his or her trust in God and not himself. Without faith it is impossible to please God. Faith is the master key to the Christian life and opens every door in your life that needs to be opened. Without genuine Bible faith you will be stranded spiritually. If you ever find yourself in faith failure, it will lead you to a place of spiritual death. Over the years I have known people, including ministers, who were once on fire for God but grew far away from God. These individuals adjusted their theology to fit their backsliding; they had a faith failure. Faith is the foundation of our Christian walk. Everything we face in life requires the faith of God (Mark 11:23-26). There are two kinds of faith: human faith and the God kind of faith. This particular subject stirs all sorts of controversy and for good reason. If a Christian ever makes this discovery and chooses to walk in the God kind of faith, their days of defeat are over.

Faith is to the Christian life what electricity is to your household appliances—nothing works without it. Faith makes everything work. You can have the best household appliances, home theater, and electronics, but without electricity you are not able to reap the benefits. If things are not working in your life, business, or ministry, it is not

God's fault. It is a faith problem. In moments like these, God's Word tells you to stir up the gift of God in you (2 Timothy 1:6-7).

Matthew 7:24-27

> *Therefore whosoever heareth these sayings of mine, and doeth them, I will liken him unto a wise man, which built his house upon a rock: And the rain descended, and the floods came, and the winds blew, and beat upon that house; and it fell not: for it was founded upon a rock. And every one that heareth these sayings of mine, and doeth them not, shall be likened unto a foolish man, which built his house upon the sand: And the rain descended, and the floods came, and the winds blew, and beat upon that house; and it fell: and great was the fall of it.*

In this Jesus story, there are two builders who had totally different building philosophies. The first man chose a rock to be the foundation for his house. The second man built his house upon the sand. Jesus had something to say about their building methods. He called the first builder wise but He gave the second builder the title of a foolish man.

Jesus gave the example in the context of teaching the people the importance of listening and obeying His words. Jesus pointed out that the wise man's house withstood the storm, but the storm demolished the foolish man's house. When Jesus said that the fall of the one house was great, He was not referring to temporal problems but rather eternal damnation. It is a serious thing to disobey the Lord.

There is nothing more serious or more horrific than to lose one's soul; it is literally beyond comprehension. The reason we have so many careless and cowardly Christians in our world today is because the foundational doctrine of eternal judgment is no longer taught in our churches. Far too many Christians do not understand the importance of "listening and obeying."

All around us we can see people whose lives are being destroyed for lack of understanding these foundational doctrines of the gospel. The temptation is to believe there is nothing we can do to help them. Yet the apostle Paul wrote that if people are blind to the light of the good news of the gospel, it is only because we are not letting our light shine:

> 2 Corinthians 4:3-4
>
> *But if our gospel be hid, it is hid to them that are lost: In whom the god of this world hath blinded the minds of them which believe not, lest the light of the glorious gospel of Christ, who is the image of God, should shine unto them.*

Light *always* overcomes darkness! If the devil seems to be winning right now, the blame belongs squarely on the Body of Christ and not sinners or the devil. We are to be a city set on a hill, allowing our light to penetrate the darkness of deception blinding the eyes of the unbelieving ones.

As I mentioned earlier, fire can be a blessing or a curse. There are demonic fires burning across our country, but there are also Holy Ghost fires beginning to burn with revival and reformation in many places, even now. The battle will be won by the fire that burns the hottest and the brightest. Leonard Ravenhill said it best, "I'm concerned in my spirit the reason the world goes to hell-fire tonight is because we (the Church) have lost Holy Ghost fire."[3]

In the Book of Revelation, we see two distinct groups. The first group is composed of overcomers. They are the company of people empowered by the Spirit of God who will successfully prevail against the forces of darkness launched against them. The other company is composed of the fearful and unbelieving. They have chosen to align themselves with the evil one and will share in his judgment.

> Revelation 21:7-8
>
> *He that overcometh shall inherit all things; and I will be his God, and he shall be my son. But the fearful, and unbelieving, and the abominable, and murderers, and whoremongers, and sorcerers, and idolaters, and all liars, shall have their part in the lake which burneth with fire and brimstone: which is the second death.*

Unfortunately, the Jesus being preached in so many pulpits today is *not* the Jesus of the Bible. Until you read the first three chapters of Revelation, you have not seen the complete picture of the real Jesus. The Jesus that came the first time as the Lamb of God will come the second time as the Lion of the Tribe of Judah. Believe me when I say, a lamb generally won't catch the attention of many people, but a lion certainly will.

> Mark 8:34-38 NLT
>
> *Then, calling the crowd to join his disciples, he said, "If any of you wants to be my follower, you must give up your own way, take up your cross, and follow me. If you try to hang on to your life, you will lose it. But if you give up your life for my sake and for the sake of the Good News, you will save it. And what do you benefit if you gain the whole world but lose your own soul? Is anything worth more than your soul? If anyone is ashamed of me and my message in these adulterous and sinful days, the Son of Man will be ashamed of that person when he returns in the glory of his Father with the holy angels."*

Prior to speaking these words, Jesus declared in Matthew 7:13-14 that the gate to Heaven is very narrow, and few will enter it; but the gate to destruction is wide, and many will choose that gate. After establishing His point, Jesus opens up a discussion about false prophets (ministers who pretend to speak in the name of the Lord). These false prophets clothe themselves as sheep, but they really are wolves in disguise. How does one discern between the true and the false minister? Jesus sets the standard! He tells us to look at the fruit that their lives and message produce. The fruit reveals the true nature of the messenger. Too many Christians broadcast and boast about their works when the Lord instructs us to look at fruit.

GIFTS VS. FRUIT

A lot of frontline Christian speakers, ministers, and pastors are given credentials, shown praise, and admired for their works, yet too many of them in these days have no godly fruit to show for their labor. In Matthew 7:21-23, Jesus offers some very sobering words:

Not every one that saith unto me, Lord, Lord, shall enter into the kingdom of heaven; but he that doeth the will of my Father which is in heaven. Many will say to me in that day, Lord, Lord, have we not prophesied in thy name? and in thy name have cast out devils? and in thy name done many wonderful works. And then will I profess unto them, I never knew you: depart from me, ye that work iniquity.

In these verses, we witness a group of people who performed great spiritual works, yet Jesus declared He never had a life of intimacy with them. Rather than being workers of righteousness, they were actually workers of lawlessness (a life not in submission to God's Word or His Spirit). This group of people then argued their case, saying they did all sorts of wonderful things in His name. They prophesied in His name, preached in His name, performed miracles in His name, and even cast out devils in His name. Their defense focused on what they did, whereas Jesus focused on their hearts. They used the name of Jesus, but they did not know the One behind the name. This reminds me of Howard Pittman's testimony when the Lord said, "You did all of that for yourself."

The people just described were not "sinners" who renounced Christ and mocked God. These were like many people today in full-time ministry who pastor churches, run large ministries, conduct evangelistic crusades, and are called on to do Christian TV programs. Jesus never said that we will know people by their works. He said we will know them by their fruit. Gifts of the Spirit are like Christmas gifts placed under the tree. It takes no effort on the part of the receiver to obtain the gift. The gift is based on the generosity of the giver who placed that gift under the tree. Here is an important point about that Christmas scene. The Christmas tree has no fruit. It exists as a showpiece for the Christmas season. It is decorated with all kinds of lights and ornaments to make the tree look beautiful, but ornaments are not to be confused with fruit.

Let me use an apple tree to make my point. It's from a very different line of trees than the varieties used for Christmas trees. The apple tree gets no flashy ornaments; it only exists to produce fruit. That apple tree is the result of being planted in good soil where it draws its life from nutrients and reaches deep to the waters that give it life. On the other hand, the Christmas tree is usually a dead tree or a fake tree used for a short season with gifts placed underneath.

In the same way, there are many in the world of Christendom who are dead or fake trees decorated with all kinds of flashy gifts and trinkets, but there is no visible fruit in their lives. The overwhelming love of God for His creation allows gifts to sometimes be placed around them for the good of the people, but those trees will be thrown into the fire one day.

> John 15:1-6 NLT
>
> *I am the true grapevine, and my Father is the gardener. He cuts off every branch of mine that doesn't produce fruit, and he prunes the branches that do bear fruit so they will produce even more. You have already been pruned and purified by the message I have given you. Remain in me, and I will remain in you. For a branch cannot produce fruit if it is severed from the vine, and you cannot be fruitful unless you remain in me. Yes, I am the vine; you are the branches. Those who remain in me, and I in them, will produce much fruit. For apart from me you can do nothing. Anyone who does not remain in me is thrown away like a useless branch and withers.*

The gifts we have are not for us but for the good of others and to be used for the glory of God. The fruit we bear is not our own. It is the result of the master gardener who prunes and purifies us so that we can produce fruit to His glory. Both the gifts He gives and the fruit He produces are for His purposes and for His glory. If a branch is severed from the life source of the vine, it can no longer produce fruit, and such branches are gathered into a pile to be burned. Faith is not merely teaching the Word of God; it is obeying the Word of God. The fruit is found in our obedience.

Having emphasized the fact that God is the giver of the gift and the fruit, we play a part in the process. God has chosen to use us in His great plans to build the Church (the Body of Christ) and to redeem the world. In 1 Corinthians 3:9-11, Paul refers to us as God's building, and then Paul identifies himself as a wise master builder. He makes it clear that there is no foundation other than Jesus Christ. We must always remember that there is a part that only God can do, and there is a part that only we can do. When God and man work in unison, His work can be completed. When that unity is broken and man decides to go his own way, there is a steep price to pay that will cost dearly.

The sixth and final foundational doctrine mentioned in Hebrews 6 is the teaching on eternal judgment. We know that God is love. That is His nature. However, there is a price to be paid if one chooses to deny and reject God and go his own way. No one could possibly live a careless life if he truly understood that he will stand before the Lord and be judged. Hebrews 9:27 states, *"It is appointed unto men once to die, but after this the judgment."*

BROKEN GATES

I taught a 20-part series from the Book of Nehemiah titled *Rebuilding the Broken Places*. It contains God's blueprint to recover and rebuild your life. If you have ever suffered loss, setback, or devastation, this is God's divine blueprint for rebuilding and regaining your life.

In this series, I present the seven strategies of opposition the enemy uses to try to stop your comeback. We see these seven strategies in the life of Nehemiah, and we watch him recognize and disable each strategy the enemy used against him. Once you identify these tactics, victory becomes possible. Nehemiah was given the impossible task of rebuilding and restoring the 10 gates of the old city of Jerusalem.

In ancient times the strength of a city's gates determined the strength of the city. Gates determined what came into the city and what was kept out. Besides the entrance to the city, gates were also a place where business was transacted, courts were convened, public policies were decided, and announcements were made. The gates of the city were the center of public activity.

American cities today do not have walls and gates as in ancient times, but there are places in our country that we can compare to the ancient gates, such as Washington, D.C., Wall Street, and Hollywood. These are the gateways into our culture. Our political systems, financial systems, entertainment centers, and educational systems determine whether our spiritual gates and walls are strong or weak. These systems have been called the seven mountains or spheres of influence. Bill Bright and Loren Cunningham were the first to speak of these mountains. Having lunch in Colorado in 1975 the Lord put on each of their hearts simultaneously the same burden. Their messages make the point that if we are to impact any nation for Jesus Christ, we must affect the seven mountains that are the pillars of society.

Ancient city walls were very tall and deep, and the gates were a place where the city elders or leaders would gather to determine policy and procedures. The parallel for modern-day America would be the laws that we pass in Congress which determine whether the gates of hell are opened or closed into our nation. When the gates—the policies and laws of our country—are based upon humanistic philosophy rather than the Word of God, then our gates are weakened, and the enemy can come in. When our laws are based upon the Word of God, the gates of Heaven are opened upon our nation, and we remain strong and secure.

Each of these gates recorded in Nehemiah is a revelation of the mind and purpose of God, and they are listed in a very specific order by God's design. The key to restoring America is to rebuild and restore each of these gates consistent with the Word of God. Our nation was founded upon godly principles, and upon these godly principles we must rebuild.

David Barton has been called "America's historian" and is the Founder and President of WallBuilders, a national pro-life, pro-family organization that presents America's forgotten history and heroes with an emphasis on our moral, religious, and constitutional heritage. In an article by David Barton titled "Is America a Christian Nation?," he points out that Barack Obama is the first American president to deny that America is a Christian nation. Then he lists quotes by other previous presidents regarding our being a Christian nation.

> The general principles on which the fathers achieved independence were....the general principles of Christianity.
>
> —John Adams

> [T]he teachings of the Bible are so interwoven and entwined with our whole civic and social life that it would be literally....impossible for us to figure to ourselves what that life would be if these teaching were removed.
>
> —Teddy Roosevelt

> America was born a Christian nation—America was born to exemplify that devotion to the elements of righteousness which are derived from the revelations of Holy Scripture.
>
> —Woodrow Wilson

> American life is builded, and can alone survive, upon...[the] fundamental philosophy announced by the Savior nineteen centuries ago.
>
> —Herbert Hoover[0]

> This is a Christian Nation.
>
> —Harry Truman[1]

The above excerpts reveal that we, as a nation, recognized and accepted our strong Christian heritage up until 2008 when we elected a president who wanted to "fundamentally transform America." What has made our country strong is when our own laws reflect God's law and not ours. Our country was built upon the laws of God. For example, most people do not realize that our three branches of government come right out of the Book of Isaiah in the Old Testament: *"For the Lord is our judge* [judicial branch], *the Lord is our lawgiver* [legislative branch], *the Lord is our king* [executive branch]*; he will save us"* (Isaiah 33:22).

America being founded upon the laws of God has made our country exceptional and stronger than any other nation in the history of the world. As we have just read, our form of government is built on Christian foundations, and these factors combined make us truly a Christian nation.

This does *not* mean that everyone in America will be a Christian. God will never force Christianity upon anyone, and neither should we. But, because of these Christian foundations, we have secured our country with very strong gates and very secure walls. Yet over the years, we have watched a gradual and steady departure from God's Word, resulting in our border walls crumbling (many are illegally pouring through our borders in unprecedented numbers) and our gates being burned (these are the political offices represented by the president, Supreme Court, and Congress).

This is not just hearsay either. An article dated October 9, 2020, in Charisma News outlined the details of how the Democratic Party made it official as to their rejection of God. In the article entitled *How the Democratic Party Divorced God and the America of 1776*, the first paragraph reads, "The Democrat Party's divorce from God has become final. In 2019, the Democrat National Committee (DNC) unanimously passed a resolution affirming atheism and declaring that neither Christianity nor any religion is necessary for morality or patriotism." In other words, "We don't need God!" Even with this bold and brazen rejection of God, many Christians and "patriots" still stand with this party. And don't think that I am here to defend the Republican party either. Some of them are actually worse than the Democrats due to their compromise and thirst for power. So many of them have put themselves up for sale to the highest bidder. I have a message entitled *Preachers, Politicians, and Principalities* that goes into greater detail and helps one understand what happens in these arenas on a spiritual plane.

The last and tenth gate in Nehemiah's time is the inspection gate, which speaks of eternal judgment. In the Bible, numbers are significant, and the number 10 is a powerful number. Ten speaks of God's government and authority. It speaks of responsibility, law and order in both divine and human structures of society. There are some biblical scholars who have said the number 10 is the number for divine perfection.

There are so many examples that show the importance of the number 10 in the Bible. Here are only a few:

The Ten Commandments

The first four commandments deal with our relationship with God, and the last six deal with our relationship with our fellow man. If the citizens of our country would adhere to these commandments, we would have to find other uses for our jails and prisons. There would be no need for them. If you go to Washington, D.C., you will see the Ten Commandments etched in stone in various places. They once held a place of honor in our culture but when we pulled the Ten Commandments out of our schools, the gates of hell opened.

The Ten Plagues

When a nation rejects the rule of God like Egypt did, putting a pharaoh in office instead of a godly leader, it will suffer the judgment of God.

The Tithe

Most of us know that the tithe is the 10 percent of our income that we give to the house of God. God set up tithing not for His good but for our good. Tithing is part of our covenant with God. I never cease to be amazed that most Christians don't get this. They nod their head how God wants to bless us financially but writhe in pain when the offering buckets go by. Money is the barometer of your heart. You can give without loving God, but you cannot love God without giving your finances to Him. Never forget that God does not need your money, and we don't make donations to God. We honor Him with the tithe. It has nothing to do with law; it has to do with love. The subject of money would require an entire book to properly delve into the topic. Israel brought a curse upon the entire nation because they withheld their tithe, and Malachi reminds us that we rob God when we withhold the tithe.

JUDGMENT AND THE FEAR OF THE LORD

At this final tenth gate, we learn that each of us will give account of the life we have lived here on earth. An inspection of our lives will be taken, unveiling all we have spoken and done. "The Hebrew verb *yare* can mean 'to fear, to respect, to reverence,' and the Hebrew noun *yirah* usually refers to the 'fear of God' and is viewed as a positive quality."[4] This fear acknowledges God's good intentions as expressed in Exodus 20:20: *"'Don't be afraid,' Moses answered them, 'for God has come in this way to test you, and so that your fear of him will keep you from sinning!'"* (NLT). Understanding this truth should bring us back to the place where the fear of the Lord is renewed. The fear of the Lord is not being afraid of God; it is reverencing, respecting, and honoring Him in all we say and do.

We will know that this gate is restored in America when the fear of the Lord has returned, and our nation has turned from its wicked ways.

Concerning the final judgment, the Scriptures speak of two judgments we should concern ourselves with: the judgment seat of Christ and the great white throne judgment. We will stand individually before God without the company of our spouses, children, pastors, or friends. At that time, there will be no secrets and no appeals court to go to. It will be an unfiltered look at every motive, attitude, and decision of our lives.

At the judgment seat of Christ, only born-again believers will appear. These people are saved and will be welcomed into the portal gates of Heaven. It is at this judgment seat where rewards will be handed out. Paul wrote to the church at Corinth saying there will be those who suffer loss in rewards, and some will make Heaven by the skin of their teeth. *"Every man's work shall be made manifest: for the day shall declare it, because it shall be revealed by fire; and the fire shall try every man's work of what sort it is. If any man's work abide which he hath built thereupon, he shall receive a reward. If any man's work shall be burned, he shall suffer loss: but he himself shall be saved; yet so as by fire"* (1 Corinthians 3:13-15).

The great white throne judgment is where the formal sentencing occurs at the end of the millennial reign of Christ. Some of the experiences that people have had as a "hell experience" were equivalent to being held in the local county jail awaiting their sentencing by a judge. From what I can tell in Scripture, it is possible that the judgment seat of Christ occurs during the seven-year Tribulation period in the earth. We will be at the marriage supper of the Lamb while the earth undergoes incomprehensible tribulation. The great white throne is at the conclusion of the millennial reign of Christ. This is the final judgment when God formally sentences satan and those who followed him, and they are cast into the lake of fire where the smoke of their torment will ascend forever and ever (Revelation 14:11).

There is nothing more serious in life than understanding this and the fact that your life must be firmly rooted in Christ. If you stand before Christ clothed in your own "righteousness," you are in trouble. If you have been born again and are standing in His righteousness, then you are saved, and you are safe.

I have had it in my heart to write a book about the subject of hell ever since I started in full-time ministry. It goes back to an experience I had as a child that served as a restraining force in my life later.

There are times and seasons for everything we do in life, and I believe I have reached the season when it is time to write that book. The Lord gave me three specific perspectives to write from, and one has to do with the personal testimony of those who have had a hell experience.

I have combed through hundreds of video and written accounts of people who claim to have had a hell experience. Some are completely delusional, and others are just completely off the wall. It is my opinion that some people have had counterfeit experiences with "angels of light" that are actually demons. Then there are those testimonies that have a ring of truth to them, and it creates a soberness in your spirit to hear them. The wacko stuff is by design from the enemy to discredit and inoculate people from hearing the truth about hell. But there is one particular testimony

I found that has impacted me more than any other. It was given by a woman from England.

She had to be one of the nicest, most sincere, credible-sounding, and proper individuals I have ever heard. She was a member of a church in England and, from what I could gather, a morally upright person with a beautiful family surrounding her.

She told the story of not feeling well one day at work and going home early. While driving to her house in foggy conditions, she had a head-on collision and found herself descending into hell. It was difficult to reconcile what I was hearing from this woman.

She was above average compared to how so many other Christians live; however, when she died, she did not see a bright white light with family members waiting for her and the overwhelming love that some have described. Instead, she went to the most horrible place imaginable, filled with fear and torment. She realized she was in hell.

As I listened to her tell how she survived this death experience, there was one sentence she spoke that I cannot forget: "No one ever told me that I had to be born again." Think about it. She was a member of a church, living a moral and upright life, but she was never told the only way into Heaven is through receiving Jesus Christ as Savior and Lord. Jesus made it clear there is only one way to the Father when He said: *"I am the way, the truth, and the life: no man cometh unto the Father, but by me"* (John 14:6).

Why Revival Tarries

Leonard Ravenhill was an English, Christian evangelist and author who lived and wrote on the subjects of prayer and revival. His book *Why Revival Tarries* is a classic and a must-read for anyone serious about seeing a genuine move of God. Ravenhill was born in 1907 in Yorkshire, England, and died in 1994 while living in Texas. He is probably best known for challenging Western evangelicalism to compare ourselves to the early Church in the book of Acts and to account for the differences.

My copy of *Why Revival Tarries* is highlighted, underlined, and complete with coffee and tear stains. I have notes scribbled throughout, and, whenever I read it, I can barely finish a page without ending up on the carpet in prayer.

His quotes are challenging and convicting, but he was unlike some who tried to write about the wrongs in the Church today, whose words ring with anger and condemnation. Ravenhill had an unusual mixture of grace, but his words were heavily laced with the two-edged sword of truth. His writings and sermons are gold mines of spiritual truth. When you read some of Ravenhill's material compared to some of the leading Christian writers of our day, it is like comparing cotton candy to a fine steak. Concerning the gospel, Ravenhill quotes, "The Gospel is not an old, old story, freshly told. It is a fire in the Spirit, fed by the flame of Immortal Love; and woe unto us, if, through our negligence to stir up the Gift of God which is within us, that fire burns low."

Once when I was in a restaurant in Scottsdale, Arizona, I ordered the best steak in the house since I love beef. I then got an education about fine beef, and it made me realize I was uninformed and had been a bit sheltered. They began to tell me about American Wagyu beef, which is known for its high quality and intense marbling. The waiter informed me that they had it available that evening for just $30 per ounce. Our waiter almost made it sound like a bargain.

I pulled out my iPhone and calculated that it was $480 per pound! WOW! I somehow missed that blue-light flashing when we entered the restaurant. What I discovered is that I just thought I knew what good steak was. That night I found out there was an entirely different level of beef that I had yet to discover. This is where we are in the world of church and ministry today, especially in America. In too many pulpits, we are being served cotton candy religion. It is real sweet and fluffy, but, when you take it in, there is no substance to it. The psalmist gives us a different recipe for good eating: *"Taste and see that the Lord is good; blessed is the one who takes refuge in him"* (Psalm 34:8 NIV).

What we call "big" in ministry here in America is not so big when compared to what God is doing around the world. Some of the largest Christian gatherings in the world have been in Nigeria (if you are into the numbers game). But it was not the numbers that impacted me in Nigeria; it was the humility of some of the leading ministers who carried the spiritual authority for the nation. In those meetings, you could feel the tangible power of God in the atmosphere. That was only the beginning. When the services began, cripples were being healed, and devils were coming out of people without a single hand being laid on them. A word of knowledge was given one evening in one of the smaller annual meetings. (There were only 2 million at this one; the larger ones usually ran in excess of 6 to 7 million.) The message was that there were witches and witch doctors present and that if they did not repent that night, they would be dead within 30 days.

My first thought was that this was a Christian gathering, not an evangelistic meeting. When a couple hundred people eventually made it up to the front and I saw people flopping around on the floor until the devils were out of them, it changed my perspective of what a powerful service can be.

Some were coming by themselves, and some were being dragged up with two or three people holding on to an arm and one holding on to their waist. What impacted me was not the wild stuff going on but people being set free from some of the worst powers of darkness you could imagine. This doesn't happen if there is not Holy Ghost fire burning somewhere.

I reflected on what we call powerful ministry, dynamic teaching and preaching in America, and realized there is an entirely different and higher level that we must reach in the Body of Christ. The reason Christians are so weak today is because they are feeding on spiritual junk food that has been overly processed and filled with artificial sweeteners and preservatives. It is nothing more than empty spiritual calories. We feel stuffed and uncomfortable after we eat some of these spiritual meals, and then we realize that we are still not satisfied. So, we head back to the spiritual fridge looking for something to satisfy us, and it generally isn't good. Spiritually we are obese and out of shape, so when really good, nutritious spiritual food is set before us, it doesn't have the appeal necessary for us to desire it or do the will of God. Too many have lost their appetite for the real food God wants to set on our plates. We hear a lot of talk and inspirational and creative sermons, but where is the substance called faith? Shouting, strutting, and animated deliveries may stir a person's soul, but it is possible the spirit man may never be touched.

Many average believers, including pastors, have no prayer life to speak of, yet the Word tells us to *"pray without ceasing"* (1 Thessalonians 5:17 NKJV). Ravenhill sums this condition up in the following way:

> No man is greater than his prayer life. The pastor who is not praying is playing; the people who are not praying are straying....We have many organizers, but few agonizers; many players and payers, few pray-ers; many singers, few clingers; lots of pastors, few wrestlers; many fears, few tears; much fashion, little passion; many interferers, few intercessors; many writers, but few fighters. Failing here, we fail everywhere.[5]

If the fire of God is to once again burn on the altars of our hearts, then we must bring the sacrifice of a surrendered life. It is a waste of time to pray for the fire to fall without offering up our lives as a living sacrifice.

AUTHORITY OF THE BELIEVER

A powerful book written by missionary John MacMillan in 1932, *The Authority of the Believer,* originally appeared as a series of articles that was later collected into a book. (You can find this free online.) There have been several books written by well-known authors regarding the authority of the believer in the past 20 to 30 years that were, no doubt, inspired by this writing.

In this book, MacMillan makes the distinction between power and authority. If we are not careful, we may find ourselves asking in prayer for more power and authority, when, in fact, every single believer already possesses power and authority. Jesus Himself said, *"Look, I have given you authority over all the power of the enemy, and you can walk among snakes and scorpions and crush them. Nothing will injure you"* (Luke 10:19 NLT).

Jesus spoke these words before He went to the cross. He was telling His disciples that the demons had to obey! After Jesus rose from the dead and before He ascended, He delivered to His disciples what we call the Great Commission, where Jesus announced that *all authority* has been given unto Him; and then He sent His disciples into all the world, equipped with power and authority. You and I are also Jesus' disciples. We also are commissioned, and we also are equipped with power and authority to get the job done!

"Ye ask, and receive not, because ye ask amiss, that ye may consume it upon your lusts" (James 4:3). If we do not

pray accurately, we simply will not receive the desired answers, and we will be continually frustrated. We can actually be praying against God's will. God is a God of order, as evidenced in His creation. Just as it is important to understand technology in order to reap the benefit of your smartphone or your computer, it is essential to have an understanding of the spiritual realm in order to get the desired results. MacMillan points out this fact, "The constitution and laws of the spiritual world are perfectly orderly and logical, and must be adhered to and carefully obeyed if the desired and promised results are to be gained."[6]

In the writings of Paul, we read how the Holy Spirit inspired this man of prayer on numerous occasions. Three of his prayers we particularly need today. Two of them are in his letter to the Ephesians and one in the letter to the Colossians. (See Ephesians 1:15-23, 3:14-21, and Colossians 1:8-14.)

In summary, Paul prayed that we as believers would have the spirit of wisdom and revelation in the knowledge of Him, that our hearts would be flooded with light so we will know the hope of His calling and see the exceeding greatness of His power. Paul tells us that we are seated together with Jesus far above all principalities and and powers, might and dominion, and *every name that is named!*

Have we become the generation that is *ever learning* but never able to get into the revelation of God's Word? I have said often that I do not blame the world for wanting nothing to do with Christianity. It's like the classic statement attributed to Gandhi, "I like your Christ; I do not like your Christians. Your Christians are so unlike your Christ." How sad!

How is it that pastors and preachers are silent about the things that really do matter, like Heaven, hell, and eternity? I'm convinced it is because we focus more of our attention on *doing* rather than *being*. In my opinion, too many of the things we are doing in "ministry" today are not the most important things. There is a vast difference between calling Jesus Lord and actually making Him Lord. When we truly make Jesus our Lord, we adopt His important priorities.

So what is most important? It's very simple. Obey the Great Commission. The Great Commission has become the Great Omission in most churches and ministries. Ninety-five percent of Christians have never led another person to the Lord; eighty percent don't consistently witness.[7] It seems that they do not care about world evangelism. Of course, American churches give money and see a few people saved, but the Great Commission must be understood from the context of the gospel of the Kingdom and not merely the gospel of salvation.

The Great Commission starts with people near you: your family, neighbors, coworkers, acquaintances, and those with whom you interact on a daily basis. In Luke 14:23, Jesus said, *"And the lord said unto the servant, Go out into the highways and hedges, and compel them to come in, that my house may be filled."* Compel them; don't just invite them.

Jesus came declaring and proclaiming the gospel of the Kingdom when He was on the earth. Do you want to know what adhering to the Great Commission looks like? Look at the life of Jesus. He was a full expression of the words He spoke to His disciples. When He commanded us to go into all the world, He meant for us to reach out to every inhabitant of the earth, the entire human family, every nation, tribe, and tongue. The Greek word for *world* means, "the ungodly multitude; the whole mass of men alienated from God, and therefore hostile to the cause of Christ."[8]

If Coca-Cola could develop a strategy to reach India with their soft drink products and within three years almost accomplish that goal, then why can't the entire Body of Christ worldwide take the gospel to the world? Coca-Cola is recognized by 94 percent of the world's population. In 2003, India doubled the retail outlets from 80,000 to 160,000, and they increased the market penetration in rural areas from 13 percent to 25 percent. India has the largest population of unreached people groups, and yet Coca-Cola is more well-known than Jesus.

We possess the majority of the wealth of the world. We possess the advantage of mass communication through today's new technology. We have training materials and capabilities beyond comprehension, and yet we still have 3 billion people who have never heard the name of Jesus.

From 1990 to 2000, more people were saved in that ten-year period than the entire previous 2,000 years. The AD2000 Project had enlisted the Body of Christ worldwide, where an estimated 100 million people were praying for world harvest. Then at the end of 2000, things seemed to just stop. I always thought it was interesting that we experienced 9/11 in 2001, and when you consider what has happened in our country, it is difficult to believe. During that ten-year window, we took the unreached people groups (UPGs) from over 16,000 down to 7,000, and now we are below the 7,000 mark of UPGs in the world.

Dr. Howard Foltz and his wife, Pat, have given their lives to the Great Commission. Linda and I have had the joy of knowing them as dear friends. We partner with them through their ministry AIMS (Accelerating International Mission Strategies, www.aims.org) to reach the unreached people groups (UPGs) in the 10/40 window.

Howard shared his testimony with me one day over a meal. At the age of 19, a missionary came to his church in Denver, Colorado, and gave an altar call. The minister said, "If you want the Lord to break your heart with the things that break His, then come forward." Howard went forward, and his life was forever changed.

Space does not permit me to share all that they have accomplished, but let me share what Howard called "God's testimony." In 1985, they founded AIMS to reach the spiritually darkest areas on the planet. The Lord has given them the grace to see 3.1 million people saved, 51,000 churches planted, and more than 170,000 pastors and leaders trained in the 10/40 window; and that number is increasing while you are reading this.[9] What I love about the strategy is that it is a church-planting strategy, churches that plant churches that plant churches and are sustained completely by the nationals who do not depend on Western money.

Howard, Pat, Linda, and I were at dinner one night when Howard summed it up so well. He said, "<u>The Great Commission must become</u> the Great Completion." We live in a time when the Great Commission is so easily within our reach, if we would just get serious about it. This is why Church For All Nations in Colorado Springs exists, to fulfill the Great Commission. It is not just something we do but why we we exist and something we continually strive to do better—to make disciples in...*Jerusalem, Judea, Samaria and the uttermost parts of the world.*

Although Dr. Howard Foltz transitioned to his heavenly reward on October 31, 2021, he left indelible marks on all those he encountered. I am one of those. I don't think I ever had a conversation with him when I did not leave more inspired and more challenged to see the Great Commission become the "Great Completion."

The vision of AIMS continues, and I am privileged to serve on its board. Our latest 2021 meeting proved to be the final board meeting with Howard in attendance, but his vision most definitely lives on.

NOTES

1. *God Is Not Great,* Atlantic Books, accessed November 29, 2021, https://atlantic-books.co.uk/book/god-is-not-great/.
2. *The Wonderful Name of Jesus,* E.W. Kenyon, Gospel Publishing, March 1, 1989, mental assent, page 42.
3. Leonard Ravenhill, source unknown.
4. Warren Baker and Eugene Carpenter, *The Complete Word Study Dictionary: Old Testament* (Chattanooga, TN: AMG Publishers, 2003), 470–471.
5. Ravenhill, *Why Revival Tarries.*
6. J. A. MacMillan, *The Authority of the Believer* (Harrisburg, PA: Christian Publications Inc.,), accessed November 30, 2021, http://www.worldinvisible.com/library/macmillan/authorityofbeliever/authority-01.htm.
7. "Evangelism Statistics," Bible.org, accessed November 30, 2021, https://bible.org/illustration/evangelism-statistics.
8. Bible Hub, s.v. "kosmos," accessed November 30, 2021, https://biblehub.com/greek/2889.htm.
9. "About Us," AIMS.ORG, accessed November 30, 2021, https://www.aims.org/about-us/.

CHAPTER 3

ARMY OF GOD RISING

Proclaim ye this among the Gentiles; Prepare war, wake up the mighty men, let all the men of war draw near; let them come up: Beat your plowshares into swords, and your pruning hooks into spears: let the weak say, I am strong. Assemble yourselves, and come, all ye heathen, and gather yourselves together round about: thither cause thy mighty ones to come down, O Lord.

Let the heathen be wakened, and come up to the valley of Jehoshaphat: for there will I sit to judge all the heathen round about. Put ye in the sickle, for the harvest is ripe: come, get you down; for the press is full, the fats overflow; for their wickedness is great. Multitudes, multitudes in the valley of decision: for the day of the Lord is near in the valley of decision.

—Joel 3:9–14

We read in Joel 1:1 that the word of the Lord came to Joel, the son of Pethuel. The name Joel signifies "Jehovah is God," or "whose God is Jehovah." In Scripture there are several Joels, but Joel the prophet is identified as *"the son of Pethuel,"* a name signifying "the sincerity of God," or "godly simplicity." It's not certain exactly when Joel prophesied, but he is generally believed to have been the earliest prophetic writer of the southern kingdom of Israel, which was Judah.[1] We have limited knowledge about Joel, but we are able to surmise that he lived in the city of Jerusalem because of references made from the texts.

Joel has insight and knowledge of the temple and the Jewish priesthood that leads us to believe he might have been a priest or the son of a priest. His writings reveal and predict an intense time of natural and national calamity for God's people. Joel uses vivid pictures of war and destruction that are sure to awaken them from the spiritual stupor that has blinded them. His prophecies begin with a word predicting a time of judgment and chastisement, as reflected in the announcement of an invasion of locusts. The goal of his prophetic message is to bring God's people to a place of repentance so they can once again experience pardon, blessing, and an outpouring of the Spirit, which will bring the final establishment of the Kingdom of God.

Isaiah creates a different theme than Joel in his prophetic proclamations. Isaiah speaks of a time of peace in chapter 2, calling on the people of Israel to beat their swords into plows and spears into pruning hooks (v. 4).

Joel, on the other hand, speaks of the day of the Lord and the coming time of war and judgment that cannot be deterred. This is certainly a reference to Armageddon, but it can also refer to our day.

Joel 3 paints a vivid picture of a clash between good and evil. In that prophetic view, Joel saw a great day coming when God will vindicate His name by judging all who have spurned Him. When we hear the phrase "the time of judgment," we conclude that it is the Lord calling for people to make a decision. Judgment is coming, and now is the time to decide who you will follow. In Joel 3:14 the prophet proclaims, *"Multitudes, multitudes in the valley of decision! For the day of the Lord is near in the valley of decision"* (NKJV).

This so references where we are in history, especially in America, with millions of people in the valley of decision. Listen to me! You cannot stand on the sidelines in this day of the Lord. You must decide: Are you with Him? Are you against Him?

In one of our prayer services in 2015, as I was leading the service from the platform, the Lord spoke to me and said there is great trouble ahead for America. As I was conversing with the Lord in my heart, I decided to pray about this later. But for some reason, the Lord wanted me to share what I heard. So I spoke this word to all of our campuses that were online with us. I sensed in my spirit that this trouble could not be stopped or avoided but could only be met head-on with faith. Little did I know that this trouble I sensed would escalate over the years and become something not easily or quickly resolved. In hindsight, I now see that the Lord was already at work in, among, and through His people. The good news is that when we meet our enemy head-on in faith, stumbling blocks become stepping-stones, and trouble can lead to our greatest triumphs. At this very moment while we are witnessing unprecedented turmoil in our world, we are also seeing a great awakening in the Body of Christ.

In Luke 22:31, Jesus tells Simon Peter that satan desires him so he can sift him like wheat to destroy him. Satan had already won a similar battle against Judas, and Jesus saw that satan was attempting to take Peter out in the same way. In the next verse, Jesus told Simon He prayed that his faith would not fail in the moment of temptation and trial.

God has a plan of redemption, but there is a spiritual battle opposing that plan, one that is intensely fervent. The resulting spiritual warfare against the saints of God cannot be avoided. It must be met head-on.

Do you wonder where we are in God's prophetic timetable? I believe we stand at a critical and pivotal moment in time. The enemies of God have gathered themselves against God and His people. We are the generation that the apostle Paul specifically wrote about in 2 Timothy 3:1–9 when he mentioned the coming of the last days. We are living in difficult and dangerous times, a time when good is called evil and evil is called good. Genuine Christianity is under siege and under persecution. A counterfeit faith has invaded the Church, resulting in the rise of an apostate church.

GOD'S MIGHTY MEN

In Joel 3:9-10, the prophet declares it is time to wake up the mighty men. It is time for warriors to take their plows and beat them into swords and turn the pruning hooks into spears. He calls on the weak to confess in faith that they are strong.

Much like in the time of Gideon, the picture on the horizon is gloomy and disturbing. We see no signs of the coming victory that has been prophesied. It seems that everywhere we turn there is a continual advance of the powers of darkness, within and without, waging war against the Body of Christ in our nation and around the globe. The temptation to respond like Gideon is present, inviting us by the winepress to wonder in fear why all of these things are happening. It took a divine encounter with God to set Gideon free from his fear and cowardice:

> Judges 6:13-14 NLT
>
> *"Sir," Gideon replied, "if the Lord is with us, why has all this happened to us? And where are all the miracles our ancestors told us about? Didn't they say, 'The Lord brought us up out of Egypt'? But now the Lord has abandoned us and handed us over to the Midianites." Then the Lord turned to him and said, "Go with the strength you have, and rescue Israel from the Midianites. I am sending you!"*

We no longer have time to strengthen ourselves with years of spiritual exercises. We must do exactly what the Lord told Gideon: *"Go with the strength you have...I am sending you!"* The Lord is with us, and that is enough. This is not the time to be discouraged and tempted to retreat.

Our strength and wisdom will not give us the victory because the arm of flesh will not save us. This is one of the great paradoxes of Christianity. There are too many in the Body of Christ who do not understand the reality and power of what appears to be a divinely illogical plan.

Let me explain. A *paradox*[2] is defined as:

1. A statement that seems to contradict itself but may nonetheless be true.
2. A person, thing, or situation that exhibits inexplicable or contradictory aspects.
3. A statement that is self-contradictory or logically untenable, though based on a valid deduction from acceptable premises.

As I was contemplating this definition, it helped me recognize and understand how the Lord works, which is so contrary to the ways of the world. The symbols of strength, power, and wisdom are the tools of the world. In God's world, He does not choose the strong and the wise. Herein lies the paradox. Christianity is not built on the strength and wisdom of man. It is built on the power and wisdom of God.

1 Corinthians 1:25-27 NKJV

Because the foolishness of God is wiser than men, and the weakness of God is stronger than men. For you see your calling, brethren, that not many wise according to the flesh, not many mighty, not many noble, are called. But God has chosen the foolish things of the world to put to shame the wise, and God has chosen the weak things of the world to put to shame the things which are mighty.

The paradoxes throughout Christianity are many. In our weakness, He is made strong; our inability becomes His ability flowing through us. As a Christian, if you really want to live, you must die. If you want to rise higher in God, you must lower yourself. If you want to find your life, you must first lose it. In order to increase, you must decrease. If you want to be first, you must be willing to be last. In order to receive, you must give. These are the characteristics of God's mighty army. It is an army of paradoxes and seeming contradictions.

If you look at the Body of Christ today, you are tempted to ask, "Where are the mighty men and women of God?" Let me assure you, they are out there! But they are not easily recognizable, and they are not exactly the ones you think they are. The group I am talking about does not need any recognition—except from Heaven. You will know if you are one of these soldiers of the Lord when you love the praise of God more than the praise of men.

Zephaniah 3:16-19

In that day it shall be said to Jerusalem, Fear thou not: and to Zion, Let not thine hands be slack. The Lord thy God in the midst of thee is mighty; he will save, he will rejoice over thee with joy; he will rest in his love, he will joy over thee with singing. I will gather them that are sorrowful for the solemn assembly, who are of thee, to whom the reproach of it was a burden. Behold, at that time I will undo all that afflict thee: and I will save her that halteth, and gather her that was driven out; and I will get them praise and fame in every land where they have been put to shame.

This scripture revealed to me a significant and essential truth that stands in contradiction to much of what we see in the Body of Christ today. We either live for the praise of men or the praise of God. God delights in those He has gathered to Himself. It is a company of misfits, it seems. He has gathered the afflicted, the lame, and the rejected ones; and He rejoices over them, breaking out in joy and praise. Finally, He says that He will get them praise and fame in the places where they have been put to shame. That is a promise!

The Old Testament reveals that every time Israel found herself at yet another impossible place, Israel cried out to God. And He showed up! He showed up in His mercy and demonstrated His grace. His mercy ensures that we do not get what we really deserve. We can count on our faithful and forgiving God. Because of our carelessness or disobedience, we deserve retribution; but His love forgives us, and His grace heals us.

Society is in disarray, our culture seems to be falling apart, and the powers of hell rage against us. But the seeming collapse of the world around us only sets the stage for God to reveal His glory in greater measure. We must remain keenly aware that the Lord is not stressed, nor is He intimidated by *anything* going on around us. He is merely waiting for us to look to Him and call upon His name. He will clothe us in His strength and show Himself strong in our behalf. He will bring down the forces of evil engaged against Him and His Church and lead us to unsurpassed victory in His name.

In Exodus 15, we find Moses's song of deliverance celebrating the awe-inspiring defeat of Pharaoh. Israel miraculously crosses the Red Sea as God divides the waters with His power. Pharaoh in his ignorance and arrogance pursues Israel to destroy her, but the Lord releases the waters, drowning the Egyptian army. There is no god like our God!

Exodus 15:3-6

The Lord is a man of war: the Lord is his name. Pharaoh's chariots and his host hath he cast into the sea: his chosen captains also are drowned in the Red sea. The depths have covered them: they sank into the bottom as a stone. Thy right hand, O Lord, is become glorious in power: thy right hand, O Lord, hath dashed in pieces the enemy.

The Lord is a man of war. He is the Lord of Heaven's armies. Never mistake His seeming delay for indifference. It is His mercy and grace that sometimes allows those delays so that His purposes might be fully accomplished. However, His delays are never denials. He does not take pleasure in the death of the wicked, but rather, He chooses to give mankind every possible chance to repent and turn toward Him. Remember that He gave Pharaoh many opportunities to repent and let Israel go. In the end, the evil ruler paid the price for his stubbornness and pride.

Right this very moment, God has His army in place all over the world. It may not look like it, but, trust me, His army is everywhere. Many of them are not yet aware they are part of the end-time army of God, but get ready! We are about to see this army rise and be fully revealed.

In spite of the fact that God is working in this army of overcomers, too much of the Church has allowed the world, rather than the Lord, to define the true nature of success for them. We were supposed to be shaping culture, but instead the culture has shaped the Church.

What we esteem so highly in the Church may in fact be abhorred by Heaven. Leaders who we have previously admired and followed in the Body of Christ have often actually been devastating failures and frauds in regard to the advancement of the Kingdom of God.

Don't Be a Successful Failure

There are two kinds of success: temporal and eternal. You can have your rewards now, or you can receive them later. Far too often, genuine moves of God that were begun in the Spirit ultimately failed because people focused on building ministries rather than advancing the Kingdom of God. Building a ministry is a temporal success at best. Yet when a person is Kingdom-minded and Kingdom-motivated, his or her work will be eternal. The Word of God provides for *good success* that will abide forever. God gave Joshua the master key to obtaining that *good* success. Here is how He described the key:

> Joshua 1:8 NKJV
>
> *This Book of the Law shall not depart from your mouth, but you shall meditate in it day and night, that you may observe to do according to all that is written in it. For then you will make your way prosperous, and then you will have good success.*

What I invest in and give my life for will create eternal rewards that bring me the greatest fulfillment and comfort. The key to Kingdom prosperity is observing the commandments of God. Through obedience, the windows of Heaven are opened.

For us to be blessed in this life is the will of God. Second Peter 1:3 says, *"His divine power has given to us all things that pertain unto life and godliness, through the knowledge of Him who has called us"* (NKJV). But we must make sure we go about it God's way. If not, we will be shortchanged and suffer great loss. Contrary to a great deal of modern-day teaching and preaching, Jesus actually taught that we are to lay up treasure for ourselves.

> Matthew 6:19 NLT
>
> *Don't store up treasures here on earth, where moths eat them and rust destroys them, and where thieves break in and steal. Store your treasures in heaven, where moths and rust cannot destroy, and thieves do not break in and steal. Wherever your treasure is, there the desires of your heart will also be.*

The Greek word for *treasure* is a word that means "deposit." As the master teacher, the Lord is teaching us how to secure our investments for eternity. No broker can offer that! God wants us to do well and prosper. Poverty is a spiritual force in the arsenal of the enemy.

In the past several years, I have met pastors, missionaries, businessmen, and others in America and around the world who belong in what I call "Faith's Hall of Fame." They recognize that their lives are not their own. They have been bought with a huge price, and they know it. They live their lives in appreciation for the price that has been paid for their spiritual freedom. They walk through life in a constant recognition that the Lord's goodness is the source of their blessing and not their own works.

These are the kind of men and women who have true Kingdom qualities of leadership. They fear and reverence

Army of God Rising

God, they love the truth, and they never allow themselves to be bribed. *"Moreover thou shalt provide out of all the people able men, such as fear God, men of truth, hating covetousness; and place such over them, to be rulers of thousands, and rulers of hundreds, rulers of fifties, and rulers of tens"* (Exodus 18:21). Washington, D.C., needs to get this message because the combination of corruption and a lack of these resolute qualities is destroying our foundations.

We have seen men and women selected to serve in our churches and ministries who have great gifts and talents, yet they do not possess these qualities. The truth is, without these characteristics in their lives, they prove to be hirelings. When the wolves come, they flee. If you can be bought, the devil will pay any price necessary to purchase your service and gain his influence over your life.

These hirelings are not the army of God that I am talking about. The real army of God is made up of ordinary people who know they serve an extraordinary God. They may not be worth anything in a world that loves the praises of men, but they are treasures in the Kingdom of God. They don't realize it, but all of the frustration, failure, and disappointments of the past years have been their boot camp, a place of divine preparation. Like the oyster that creates a beautiful pearl through a painful irritation, they are emerging as vessels who have been prepared for this very time. Quite soon you will see this army of God rising to gather the final end-time harvest.

THE PRESENCE OF GOD

The key to victory in these days is not the power of the flesh but the presence of our God. What makes this army something to be feared is not the individual soldiers in the army but the presence of God in their midst. Security is not the absence of danger but the presence of God—no matter what the danger. The arm of flesh will always fail (Jeremiah 17:5); God takes great measures to teach us this valuable truth. The Word of God makes it clear that every great man or woman of God must go through an "emptying process" in order to be used by God.

Moses's school of preparation was a 40-year stint on the backside of the desert. Before he entered that place to be used by God, he had been schooled in all the wisdom of the Egyptians and was a great orator and producer of great deeds. But when God had finished his training program, he could not even carry on a decent conversation! One Jewish Rabbi described that dramatic change in Moses with these words, "When Moses says, 'Who am I that I should go to Pharaoh?' God answers not by telling Moses who he is, but by telling him who God is, saying 'I will be with you' (Exodus 3:12)."[3]

After you have been in the school of the Lord and He has you prepared to serve Him, you may feel totally inadequate to do anything at all. That seems to be the story of my life. If you are full of yourself, there is no room for Him. Pride is the armor of darkness, and lies are what hold it in place. There is nothing greater or more powerful than truth and nothing weaker than lies. One of the greatest breakthroughs you can ever experience is to recognize how utterly helpless you are apart from God. However, as Paul says in Philippians 4:13, you can do all things through Christ who strengthens you.

God's presence in our midst is our victory. Psalm 9:3 says it this way, *"When my enemies are turned back, they shall fall and perish at thy presence."* The sign of the presence of God in the Old Testament was the ark of the covenant (also known as the ark of His presence). Over and over again, when the ark was taken onto the battlefield, Israel was victorious.

The ark of the covenant gives us clues as to how to gain the victory assured us.

The ark of the covenant was simply a wooden box 45 inches long, 27 inches wide, and 27 inches high that was overlaid with gold inside and out. The wood speaks of our humanity, and the gold speaks of our faith and His divinity. When Israel had the ark in their midst, they won their battles; but when they allowed the ark to be captured by their enemies, they suffered tragic loss.

Within the ark were three items of key significance:

- The tablets of stone: On these tablets were inscribed the Ten Commandments, which represent our covenant with The Lord and the written Word of God.
- Golden pot of manna: This speaks of the Word of God that is quickened to us by the Holy Spirit, or what we often call the *rhema,*

as opposed to the *logos*. The *logos* is the written Word of God, but the *rhema* is a quickened word from God.

- Aaron's rod that budded: This was an old dry almond tree branch that speaks of the power of God's anointing upon us and the ability to bear fruit instantly.

Within the ark, we find the mystery and the reality of what makes great men and women of God. They are people of the Word, which focuses on three things in order to reap the full benefit God intends: you must read the Word, study the Word, and meditate on the Word. It must reach the place in your life where it becomes the meditation of your heart that will, in turn, become *rhema*. This sets the stage for the presence of God to be upon you, which is the anointing that destroys the yoke (Isaiah 10:27).

Ministers of God's Word cannot depend on their own abilities or their own personalities. The day of the rock-star minister is over. We have had our idols in leadership far too long, and it has prevented people in the world from meeting the real Jesus. There is a "spirit" that can come upon leaders that can kill a move of God and transform it from a living reality into a dead monument. Yes, God uses men, and we give honor where honor is due, but that honor should never be the cause of pride. There is a serious responsibility upon leadership to keep His presence paramount in all that we do in His name. Our success is not about men's greatness; it is about the Holy Spirit's presence in our midst.

Remember Gandhi allegedly said that he really liked our Christ, but he did not like Christians because they were so unlike their Christ. We should read those words and weep. It is His presence that causes mountains to move. If we were a people determined to walk in the presence of God, we would see others drawn to His presence—not to us. In Revelation 6, when men refused to repent of their evil and wickedness, they ran from His presence into the caves, *"and said to the mountains and to rocks, 'Fall on us and hide us from the presence of Him who sits on the throne, and from the wrath of the Lamb! For the great day of their wrath has come, and who is able to stand?'"* (Revelation 6:16-17 NKJV). They did this in order to not look upon the face of the King of kings and Lord of all lords.

> 2 Corinthians 2:15-16 NKJV
>
> *For we are to God the fragrance of Christ among those who are being saved and among those who are perishing. To the one we are the aroma of death leading to death, and to the other the aroma of life leading to life.*

ARMY OF GOD RISING

There is, however, an army of God rising. It may not look like it, but there are mighty men and women of God everywhere who have been in wilderness training for many years. They are being prepared to be released for what the Lord is about to do. As I mentioned earlier, many in this army are not aware of it. Yet as you are reading this, I believe that *you* are one of those called to be in the army of the Lord. You may not recognize this to be true, but let me offer this point.

The United States Armed Forces is believed by many to be the most sophisticated military power in the world. I share this belief, yet I have often said that does not make us better or more valuable than other nations, but it does place a greater responsibility upon us. I'm so proud of our soldiers and so very thankful for them every day. But the one thing that we as a nation must never forget is the grace of God that is upon us. It is only the blessing of the Lord upon us that truly makes us the most powerful nation in the world (Psalm 33:12).

In spite of this, there have been numerous times our political leadership has not released our military to do their job, especially soldiers in times of war. They have held them back with their hands tied and even betrayed our own people. Yet, our military is still one of the best, and they willingly go into battle and lay down their lives for a greater cause that transcends the will of our weakened political system and corrupt leaders.

When God envisions His army, Gomer Pyle is not what He had in mind. Some of you may remember the hit comedy from the 1960s, *Gomer Pyle: USMC*. Gomer was hardly the poster child representing America's finest; his TV character didn't represent someone ready and able to go to battle. Too much of the Body of Christ appears like a Gomer Pyle that is no threat to the enemy. The apostle Paul paints a picture in his letter to the church at Corinth about the man or woman God has prepared for war against the enemy.

The Corinthian church was a mess. They had all the gifts of the Spirit operating, but they were carnal and filled with strife and division. There was also some serious sin in the camp. Paul may well have experienced more grief with this group than any other. Actually, some scholars believe Paul wrote a "severe letter" or very serious rebuke to the Corinthian church that did not make it into the Bible.

In his first letter to that gifted but disorderly church, Paul gives the definition of the type of person God can use in the day of the Lord. That definition will come as a surprise.

> 1 Corinthians 1:26-29 NLT
>
> *Remember, dear brothers and sisters, that few of you were wise in the world's eyes or powerful or wealthy when God called you. Instead, God chose things the world considers foolish in order to shame those who think they are wise. And he chose things that are powerless to shame those who are powerful. God chose things despised by the world, things counted as nothing at all, and used them to bring to nothing what the world considers important. As a result, no one can ever boast in the presence of God.*

Think about this. The Greek word for *foolish* is where we get the word *moron*. In other words, this army that God is about to release on the powers of hell is not your typical army. They are a ragtag group of men and women who may appear weak and foolish compared to the world's standards. There is nothing threatening about them. Nevertheless, this is exactly how God chooses to show forth His power; in doing so, He gets the glory. He uses the most unlikely and simple people to accomplish amazing things in the Kingdom of God. A dear pastor friend of mine says it this way, "Have you ever noticed that God allows the odds to get stacked against His people and puts them in impossible situations so that there is no human explanation for victory. Then, when He shows up we get the victory, and He gets the glory." It is also important to understand that if you are educated, wealthy, and highly gifted, you also can be used of God. Pride is the issue at hand, and pride will disqualify you.

The writers of the Bible did not erase from their writing the faults and weaknesses of men and women the Lord used to accomplish His purposes. Joshua battled such fear and discouragement that the Lord had to continually remind him not to be afraid or dismayed. Gideon was discouraged and hiding out in fear when the Lord summoned him as a *"mighty man of valor"* (Judges 6:12 NKJV).

Samson could well be the greatest type and shadow of the Church in the Old Testament. His life and story certainly reveal our human weakness and ineffectiveness. The story of Samson ranks as one of the most well-known stories in the Bible. He was raised up by God to serve as one of the judges in Israel, and he was destined to deal with the never-ending problem of the warmongering

Army of God Rising

Philistines. After the Israelites were delivered from the tyranny of the Philistines by Jephthah, Israel again fell back into their evil ways.

As a result of their bad choices, Israel remained in bondage to their enemies for 40 years. At the end of that time, an angel of the Lord appeared to the wife of Manoah of the tribe of Dan and told her that she would give birth to a son who would deliver Israel from the weight of the oppression caused by the Philistines. The Babylonian rabbis knew Manoah's wife as Zlelponi. Along with that announcement, the angel gave her clear instructions on how her son, Samson, should be raised. Both mother and child would take a vow of abstinence from all things intoxicating and unclean. Along with that, Zlelponi was instructed that Samson should never cut his hair, as it would be the secret to his strength. This vow is called the Nazarite vow.

Hair in the Bible can be a type and shadow of the gifts of God, wherein lies our strength and influence. Absalom, the rebellious son of David, had such incredibly beautiful hair that they would cut it once a year and weigh it. One of my Bible references said that there was potentially five pounds of hair in one cutting. But, sadly, the gift that lifted him up was the very thing the enemy used to take him down. Absalom died an ignominious death when his hair was caught in a tree while fleeing from his dad. Although the story of Samson is one big carnival of symbols, it also clearly illustrates we must never allow the gifts that God

117

gives us to become the weapon the enemy uses to take us out.

Samson's life could be characterized as a life of faith and folly. There were failures in his life, beginning with his seduction by Philistine women. Samson broke off from the ways of a Nazarite and allowed himself to be seduced and then betrayed by these unfortunate choices in women. Samson did not abstain from the enticements of the world and women as he was instructed. Eventually, Delilah was his final downfall. Her seduction was devious, and her cooperation with Philistine leaders brought down the mighty Samson. Samson allowed Delilah, who represents the world, to capture his attention and take his eyes off of God. As the story goes, while Samson had his head in Delilah's lap, she discovered the secret to his strength was his hair.

Right here, we see the danger of a sleeping Church! While Samson slept, his hair was cut. When he awoke, he had no strength to resist the Philistines; they bound him, took him down to the prison house, gouged out his eyes, and tied him to the grinding stone. (See Judges 16:1-22.)

Samson was not bound by just any chains. He was bound by chains of brass, which speak of judgment. Like Samson, too many in the Body of Christ have lost their strength and found themselves in a prison house forced to work at the grinding wheel, going in circles accomplishing little to nothing for the Kingdom of God. We have been a mockery to the world. Sadly, many high-profile Christians have become the source of great shame and joke material for late-night comedians because of their foolish behavior and disobedience.

Army of God Rising

Even more shocking, if you ask most people in the Body of Christ today for a status report, they think we are doing so well and that there is nothing wrong in the Church. Unfortunately, too many are somewhat like the Laodicean Church, shamelessly asserting, *"[We are] rich, and increased with goods, and have need of nothing."* Yet the Lord had a completely different opinion when He said that they were *"wretched, and miserable, and poor, and blind, and naked"* (Revelation 3:17). Wow! How does that happen? How could we be so wrong in our assessment of who we are and where we are?

Fortunately, this story of shame and failure does not end there. Failure is not necessarily final! Even while Samson was going in circles, blind and mocked by his enemies, something was happening—something supernatural. Samson's hair was growing back.

Unaware that God was at work and Samson's hair was regrowing, the Philistines decided to throw a party. While the Philistines worshipped their false god, Samson, a type of the Church, would be the source of their entertainment. But this enemy was unaware of a glorious truth! God can redeem any situation, no matter how tragic, and turn it into a glorious victory.

In the same manner, the Church today in many places has been going in circles at the grindstone, blinded and bound by the enemy. And yet, all the while, our "hair" has been growing; our strength is coming back! The power of God is reviving the Church, and, by His presence, we can and will win the battles we face.

As the Philistine rulers continued their celebration that day long ago, offering sacrifices and praises to their god, Dagon, God was at work. Here is a little peek into that celebration party.

> Judges 16:23–25 NLT
>
> *The Philistine rulers held a great festival, offering sacrifices and praising their god, Dagon. They said, "Our god has given us victory over our enemy Samson!" When the people saw him, they praised their god, saying, "Our god has delivered our enemy to us! The one who killed so many of us is now in our power!" Half drunk by now, the people demanded, "Bring out Samson so he can amuse us!" So he was brought from the prison to amuse them, and they had him stand between the pillars supporting the roof.*

In those ancient times, it was not out of the ordinary for the heathen people to celebrate their victories in a most heathen way. It was a common practice for them to haul in their prisoners of war before all the people and make a mockery of them—ridiculing, jeering, and scorning them. While they would heap upon these prisoners every form of indignity, they offered grateful tribute to their gods, who they recognized for giving them aid in triumphing over their enemies.

> Judges 16:26–30 NLT
>
> *Samson said to the young servant who was leading him by the hand, "Place my hands*

against the pillars that hold up the temple. I want to rest against them." Now the temple was completely filled with people. All the Philistine rulers were there, and there were about 3,000 men and women on the roof who were watching as Samson amused them.

Then Samson prayed to the Lord, "Sovereign Lord, remember me again. O God, please strengthen me just one more time. With one blow let me pay back the Philistines for the loss of my two eyes." Then Samson put his hands on the two center pillars that held up the temple. Pushing against them with both hands, he prayed, "Let me die with the Philistines." And the temple crashed down on the Philistine rulers and all the people. So he killed more people when he died than he had during his entire lifetime."

This building seems to have been similar to the spacious and open amphitheaters, well known among the Romans and still found in many countries of the East. There were two sections where people could be entertained by this contempt and ridicule of Samson. There was the customary seating section, probably for the wealthier citizens, and the upper roof. The whole edifice rested upon two pillars and rose on an inclined plane, providing a view of the center area to everyone. Samson was brought before them with his sightless eyes and flailing arms, trying to protect himself.

It was at that point Samson cried out to the Lord. He turned from trusting in his own strength to acknowledge the God of Israel as his source of strength. Faith was renewed and courage returned. He asked a young man to position him between the two pillars holding up the temple seating area. He then prayed and asked God to give him strength one more time so he could defeat the enemies of Israel. God answered that prayer, and strength flooded into every muscle of his body. With one great push, Samson brought down the whole house, killing 3,000 Philistines and himself. More people were killed in Samson's death than in his life.

When the Church begins to realize that our power comes from the Lord and not ourselves, victory can be gained. When we choose to die to ourselves and lose our lives for His glory, then we will regain vision for the purpose of the Body of Christ on the earth. We will take more in our death to self than all the previous years of our lives when we truly place our faith in the Greater One.

God's Boot Camp

God's boot camp is not always conventional or to our liking. Abraham was told to leave his father and the comforts and safety of his inheritance and follow God to a land promised to him. Instead of leaving his extended family behind, Abraham dragged them all along, and, to the best of our knowledge, this delayed the plan of God by at least five years. Abraham was told not to fear but to trust God. Yet, all along the journey, there was stumbling and fumbling faith. Around 25 years later, he finally entered into the promise of God. It was there that he was *fully persuaded* of the beauty of God's wonderful plan for his life.

This training of the saints is unceasing. We come to Abraham's son, Isaac. There was a time when Isaac was faced with a dilemma. The Philistines were envious of the favor that seemed to be upon his life, so they filled in with dirt all the wells his father Abraham had dug.

We see this happening in our day in a spiritual way. The wells of our spiritual fathers also have been stopped up and can no longer supply the refreshing living waters God intended. The well of the spirit of faith, the gifts of the Spirit, healing, prosperity, world missions, and other wells have been stopped up by doubt, distraction, thoughtlessness, and fear. We live in a time when we must re-dig the ancient wells. Isaac apparently did some re-digging, and the well of faith was opened up in a powerful way. Isaac sowed good seed in a time of famine and reaped a hundredfold return in the same year (see Genesis 26:12).

Jacob spent a great deal of time in God's training school. It started at birth and lasted almost his whole life. He was the consummate con man, using deceit to get what he wanted. Eventually, the con man was conned by Laban. Jacob spent 14 years in a Holy Spirit training camp, learning to trust God. He was desperate for the blessing of God and even found himself wrestling an angel.

Though he had serious character flaws, his life was finally changed. That encounter with the angel left him walking with a limp, which would serve as a constant reminder of his own weakness. The change in his life was so powerful he would eventually undergo a name change. He went from being Jacob, the deceiver, to Israel, the prince of God. No longer did he play the con game because he finally got to the place his trust was in God. There are a lot of Jacobs in our nation. They are in jails and rehabilitation places, and they often keep wrestling with God, who will not give up until He prevails in their lives. Even in those places, God has some Isaacs and some Jacobs ready to be transformed by the power of God.

Joseph was the ultimate example of the power of the school of the Lord. He was a dreamer, but his dreams caused his family to want to kill him and ultimately landed him in an Egyptian prison. And just when it looked like it couldn't get any worse, it did. He endured 13 years of serious hardship before he ended up in the palace where he belonged. His obedience during incredible suffering and hardship allowed God to prepare him to be used to save an entire nation. The life of Joseph teaches us a powerful lesson: when you are down to nothing, God is most certainly up to something great.

David was a man after God's own heart. As a teenager he slew Goliath and initiated victory for the people of Israel. Yet instead of King Saul appreciating what David accomplished, he created situations that kept David on the run and fighting for his life for years. David and his men were discouraged, distressed, deeply in debt, and at one point, hiding from Saul and his army. This is the school of learning in which David found himself. It wasn't supposed to be like this. Samuel had promised that he would be king, yet here he was living like a vagabond. In the end, David prevailed, and those men who stood with him gained notoriety as David's mighty men.

David lived to become Israel's greatest king. However, he was not without some serious character flaws. His lust for Bathsheba led him down a dark road of sin and failure. He made some really bad decisions, and it cost him. In the end, David repented and turned his heart back to God. In spite of his sins and numerous mistakes, he continued to follow the Lord. He walked through the dark night of his many failures and finally came back into the light of the Father's presence.

Hopefully, you can find comfort in identifying with great men and women of God in the Bible who sinned but were still used of God. At the same time, be warned that you can permanently alter your life with sin. Yes, it is true that the Lord will continue to love you, but sin is deadly, and its consequences can permanently and horribly alter your life. Remember the saying, "Sin will take you farther than you want to go, keep you longer than you want to stay, and cost you more than you want to pay." Avoid sin like the plague, and do not resist the Lord's desire to heal you and free you from your own weaknesses and the deceitfulness of your heart.

In Jeremiah 17:9, we read these words, *"The human heart is the most deceitful of all things, and desperately wicked. Who really knows how bad it is?"* (NLT).

As we walk through times of darkness and failure, we often misunderstand and misalign ourselves, meaning we misalign ourselves with the wrong people, people who support us in our descent into making wrong decisions, and we may misunderstand what it means that God can redeem all that we have lost in our moments of running from Him. Hardship and pain are the arenas in which our character can be shaped and forged into a weapon for good. Don't waste your sorrow by trying to circumvent what God is trying to do in you while you are in your own prison of pain. Submit yourself to God, and let Him heal your heart and change you in those times of failure and adversity.

God has a school of the Spirit that He intends for us all to enter. But it seems most people drop out, and few ever graduate. Learning this truth will put you in the class of Paul, who discovered this great truth and began to rejoice during his times of betrayal, hardship, and persecution. In Romans 5:3-5 he writes,

"We can rejoice, too, when we run into problems and trials, for we know that they help us develop endurance. And endurance develops strength of character, and character strengthens our confident hope of salvation. And this hope will not lead to disappointment. For we know how dearly God loves us, because he has given us the Holy Spirit to fill our hearts with his love" (NLT).

It is not circumstances that make or break you; they simply introduce you to yourself. It is how you react to those trials that determines your outcome in the school of the Spirit. How you respond in the day of trouble and tragedy is what propels you to true greatness or drags you into the pit.

A great book that illustrates the path of training for all of God's soldiers is *The Tale of Three Kings* by Gene Edwards. In his incredible storytelling style, Edwards introduces us to three kings: David, the shepherd king; Saul, the jealous king; and Absalom, the rebellious son. Their stories reveal two kinds of leadership in the Body of Christ: leaders with a shepherd's heart and abusive leaders who take advantage of the people. But this book is much more than an examination of leadership styles. At the very core of the book is a study on brokenness.

In chapter 5, Edwards makes a very powerful point:

> God has a university. It's a small school. Few enroll; even fewer graduate. Very, very few indeed. God has this school because he does not have broken men and women. Instead, he has several other types of people. He has people who claim to have God's authority...and don't—people who claim to be broken...and aren't."[4]

Brokenness is not a negative thing; it is a very positive and important characteristic of the believer. In Matthew 5:3, Jesus points out that those who are poor in spirit are vessels who manifest Heaven through them. In Scripture, the horse represents spiritual warfare, and one of the 10 gates that had to be restored in Nehemiah's time was the horse gate, representing spiritual warfare. You cannot take a horse that has not been broken into battle.

In *A Tale of Three Kings,* Edwards shows how critical our responses to life are. They determine the measure of brokenness we will experience in life and what our future will be.

Probably most of us, at one time or another, have lived under a Saul-type leadership. It tests us, frustrates us, and breaks us; and in the end, it can remove the potential Saul in us. We don't want to become like Saul, who is jealous of another's success rather than rejoicing with them. Like Saul, jealousy and competition will embitter you and destroy you.

Absalom-type leaders seek to grab what they have not earned. I have experienced the pain and betrayal of numerous spiritual sons who became an Absalom. It is gut-wrenching to watch someone destroy his destiny and the lives of so many other people. But rather than get bitter, I chose to get better. God made even this work for my good to become a better spiritual father. I saw this as part of my preparation for that which God has ultimately called me into.

At some time or another, we all find ourselves like David. He would not allow Saul's treachery and attacks to embolden him to engage in self-pity and revenge. Neither do we want to be like David who was so blinded by sin that it took a person like Nathan, the prophet, to confront him. Even in that, David repented and proved the genuineness of his broken heart.

If you have ever studied the great achievers in history, you will find that the majority of their lives are spent in preparation for what they are really destined to do. Life is their real training ground, not the university or the seminary.

A successful businessperson was once asked what his key to success in life was, and he responded, "Massive failure." Bad judgment and critical mistakes can be the keys that unlock the door to success in life. In life, these achievers have learned that stumbling blocks become stepping-stones to the next level. Edison once said that he had never failed trying to invent the light bulb; he just found 10,000 ways it did not work. One viewpoint of success is going from failure to failure without losing enthusiasm. Failure is the thing you encounter on the way to victory.

Don't miss your day of preparation! Treasure your challenges and hardships, knowing that there is a reward for those who never give up. Let the pressures that you are enduring shape you from the inside out into what God has designed you to be. It takes courage to never give up in the face of failure. But God's mighty warriors are courageous people who never, ever give up.

It Takes Courage

If there were ever a time when we needed courage, it is now. But let me be clear: Courage is a choice and not a feeling. I have heard it said that, "Courage is not the absence of fear; it is the mastery of it." Fear is the barrier we must all break through, and it is courage that leads the way. Life shrinks or expands with the degree of your courage.

Courage is not natural. But you can grow courage by spending time in the presence of the Lord. Psalm 27:14 says, *"Wait for the Lord; be strong and take heart and wait for the Lord"* (NIV).

The world is waiting to see the rise of men and women of great courage who are willing to take on the forces of evil. This is why David, a teenage shepherd boy with no formal training in warfare, was able to slay Goliath. Goliath was trained in warfare from his youth and was such a physically imposing figure that he had all of Israel in fear. When David heard him ranting against Israel and cursing their God, he got fired up. It was courage and confidence in his God that led young David to the battlefield that day.

While Goliath had everyone else trembling, David was thinking, "I need to take this guy out. Who does he think he is to defy my God?" What was David's secret? He spent time with his God. He walked and talked with his God. He was a worshipper who cherished the presence of God. David was so intoxicated with God's presence that all he could see was how big his God was and how small Goliath was by comparison.

If you look at the problems in this world through natural eyes, you will conclude it is impossible to change the direction our country and culture are headed. Yet if you look at things through the eyes of faith, there are no problems, only God solutions. The human spirit is designed to conquer and overcome; the believer is built for exploits, and victory will be ours as we are intimate with God. *"And such as do wickedly against the covenant shall he corrupt by flatteries: but the people that do know their God shall be strong, and do exploits"* (Daniel 11:32).

People are attracted to courageous people and choose to follow them—sometimes even in the wrong direction.

Army of God Rising

That's why now is the time to demonstrate who we are in Christ and manifest the courage God has given us so people can choose to follow the right direction. When we stand up and speak up, people will be drawn to us and find their own courage to follow the Lord. *"When they saw the courage of Peter and John and realized that they were unschooled, ordinary men, they were astonished and they took note that these men had been with Jesus"* (Acts 4:13 NIV).

If you ever face a time when you feel far from God, there is a simple fix: draw near to Him. There is an incredibly powerful and rich promise that the Lord gives us in James 4:8, *"Come close to God, and God will come close to you. Wash your hands, you sinners; purify your hearts, for your loyalty is divided between God and the world"* (NLT). If you want to walk closely with the Lord, all you need to do is draw near to Him. When you do that, He promised He will draw near to you. If you feel like you are far from God, guess who moved? It isn't God.

So the question is, "How do you become intimate with the Lord?" James admonished us to wash our hands and purify our hearts. He was using old covenant terminology to express a new covenant concern for the condition of the heart. Intimacy begins in the heart and requires a clean heart for residence.

Under the law, priests were commanded to cleanse their hands and feet at the laver before drawing near to God in the holy place (Exodus 30:18-20). The washing of one's hands signifies the cleansing of one's actions, while the washing of one's feet designates the cleaning of one's life in a daily walk with God.

The ceremony of water baptism in the temple represented a vow of obedience, and the participant promised a change of lifestyle and habits. In the New Testament, we are buried with Him in the waters of baptism and raised to walk in the newness of life in Christ. In taking this step of obedience, we choose to adopt His standard of righteousness that is possible when we are in Christ.

When Paul was writing to the church at Corinth, which was acting out in such carnal ways, he asked them the question, "Who is able to be God's counselor?" The obvious answer is absolutely no one. Yet, he concludes that we possess the mind of Christ! We access His mind through meditating on the Word of God and listening to the Holy Spirit. *"For who hath known the mind of the Lord, that he may instruct him? but we have the mind of Christ"* (1 Corinthians 2:16).

As we read, study, and meditate on the Word of God, we begin to walk in a supernatural intelligence the world doesn't even know exists. I have heard it said, "There is no mountain anywhere; every man's ignorance is his mountain." When we are ignorant of what God says about any part of our lives, we will always pay a huge price.

God has given unto us everything that pertains to life and godliness, but it resides in the form of the promises of God. While God's love is unconditional, His promises are not. There are conditions placed upon them. What are those conditions?

First, you must believe and not doubt. To not doubt means you will not withdraw from what God has promised. Your mind may be assaulted with doubts, but you do not have to accept them. If you are going to doubt, then doubt your doubts, and believe God.

Secondly, you must act according to what you believe. Faith without works is dead. When the Bible says that the joy of the Lord is our strength, we must keep and protect our joy. According to Galatians 5:22, joy is a spiritual force, unlike happiness, which is primarily a soulish power. Joy cannot be quenched if we choose to walk in the Spirit. Even after the disciples were severely beaten and bleeding in Acts 5:40-41, they went their way rejoicing that they were counted worthy to suffer for His name's sake. You cannot stop the men or women of God when they get a hold of this truth. Faith in action is not fragile and will not cave in at the slightest hint of opposition.

There is an interesting message in James 1:8: *"A double minded man is unstable in all his ways."* In the opening treatise of his letter, James unveils what causes instability in the life of the believer. It is a double mind—a mind that is different and contrary to the mind of Christ. When your mind is in competition with the mind of Christ, it creates uncertainty. James is saying that a double-minded person has two natures within him: the mind of the flesh and the mind of the spirit or the new creation. Each person has a mind of his own, but a double-minded person is someone trying to go in two entirely different directions at the same time.

It is only as we put to death the old man, our fleshly nature, that we can become single-minded. A dead man has no mind of his own. You cannot offend a dead man. Paul presents this spiritual secret in Romans 6:11, *"Likewise reckon ye also yourselves to be dead indeed unto sin, but alive unto God through Jesus Christ our Lord."*

Could it be that our lack of boldness and courage is due to a lack of personal relationship with the Lord and His Word? One thing I do know is: If you draw near to God, He will draw near to you. You cannot be living in God and at the same time be suffering stagnation, weakness, or discouragement.

"Great peace have they which love thy law: and nothing shall offend them" (Psalm 119:165). There is a place in God that we must strive to enter; it is called the rest of the Lord. When we love His Word, we enter into the place where nothing can offend us, ensnare us, or cause us to stumble. This is the walk of the Spirit. This is the rest of God.

If you find yourself in the pit like Joseph, there are powerful things happening that can cause you to rejoice. Did I say rejoice? Yes, I did.

- The pit is where you learn to trust God and not men.
- The pit is where you discover what is really inside you.
- The pit is where you crucify your flesh.
- The pit is where God will pour steel into your soul.

- The pit is where you learn to sing a song even in the midnight hour like Paul and Silas did (Acts 16:25).

The pit is what prepares you for the palace. A mushroom can spring up overnight, but an oak tree will take many years.

Who you are is not always seen by others, but it is noticed in the spirit world. Whether it is laziness, compromise, diligence, courage, or any other trait, it is seen by both demons and angels.

> Acts 19:13-16 NLT
>
> *A group of Jews was traveling from town to town casting out evil spirits. They tried to use the name of the Lord Jesus in their incantation, saying, "I command you in the name of Jesus, whom Paul preaches, to come out!" Seven sons of Sceva, a leading priest, were doing this. But one time when they tried it, the evil spirit replied, "I know Jesus, and I know Paul, but who are you?" Then the man with the evil spirit leaped on them, overpowered them, and attacked them with such violence that they fled from the house, naked and battered.*

Here is a challenging thought for those of us in ministry and in what we call the fivefold ministry (apostle, prophet, evangelist, pastor, or teacher). Consider what your ministry is and how and where you minister on a normal weekly basis. Ask yourself if your ministry would continue if you did not have your building, sanctuary, congregation, or class where you minister.

Preachers, what if your platform, lights, videos, organ, keyboard, or choir were not behind you anymore? What would you do if Christianity were suddenly illegal and churches were closed down and persecution increased to such a degree that anyone professing Christ would be severely persecuted? We actually saw this to a certain degree in America on March 15, 2020. I pulled into an empty parking lot, and the only cars there were some of our staff and worship and media teams. We must ask ourselves: would the Kingdom of God continue to advance through our ministries, our churches, and ourselves? For me, this is a serious question, and I am presently asking this of myself and making the appropriate adjustments in order to train our staff and our people to be true disciples of the Lord, no matter what happens in our country.

It is a verifiable fact throughout history that persecution has been one of the best things for the spread of the gospel. Trouble and opposition cannot stop the advancement of the Kingdom. It usually brings out the best in true believers and the worst in marginal believers.

Both Judas and Peter denied the Lord, but one is in Heaven, and one is in hell right now. Peter was wobbly in his faith, but he repented. Peter went on to become a pillar in the Church due to the prayers of the Lord on his behalf.

Before His crucifixion, Jesus was shown that satan saw something in Peter that he thought could take him out, so

Army of God Rising

Jesus prayed and interceded for him that his faith would not fail. He did not pray to bind the devil. He prayed that Peter's faith would not fail, because faith is the victory that overcomes the world.

Peter had a great heart and thought he was strong. He told the Lord he would never forsake Him and that he would die for Him. But when the hour of trial came, Peter vehemently denied the Lord three times and with cursing.

Peter could not blame that little incident on his boss (Jesus). Many people who look at their own failure never place the responsibility where it genuinely belongs—on themselves. They live in a world of victim mentality that prevents them from taking personal responsibility. Unless they overcome that victim mentality, they can never grow up spiritually.

People say things such as, "I grew up in an abusive home with an abusive father, oppressive mother, dysfunctional family, poor family, rough neighborhood, etc." The list goes on. Of course, we have great compassion for those who have suffered and endured these hardships. But the real truth of the matter is that we cannot be a victor and a victim at the same time. God is eager to heal us from the past, and we must let Him.

Adam and Eve had a perfect Father, a beautiful paradise for their environment and home, and no sin nature to battle against. In spite of making their home in a perfect place, they sinned and sent the entire human race plunging into spiritual and physical death. With nothing but absolute perfection around them, the first thing Adam did was blame his wife! In effect, he blamed the Lord when he said, *"It's that woman you gave me, Lord!"* (See Genesis 3:12). Instead, Adam should have taken personal responsibility.

Husbands and wives, children, and Christian brothers and sisters, if you are not able to resist blaming, arguing, and fighting with one another, how will you ever stand strong in the day of battle? How would you respond if you were told to deny the Lord or face jail time or death? Our Middle Eastern brothers and sisters in the Lord face harsh conditions like these on a daily basis.

This is the day of the Lord. An army has been prepared that is ready to take its place on the battlefield. These are men and women of faith and courage. They know the way of brokenness and have refused to give in to a victim mentality. Who are they? Where are they? Well, they are about to be revealed, and you just might be shocked to discover who is in this band of warriors. They are seemingly insignificant people, but they are the rising army of God.

Notes

1. Bible Hub, "Joel 1:1," accessed November 30, 2021, https://biblehub.com/commentaries/joel/1-1.htm.
2. *The American Heritage® Dictionary of the English Language*, 5th Edition.
3. Harold S. Kushner, *Overcoming Life's Disappointments* (New York: Anchor Books, 2007), 14–15.
4. Gene Edwards, *A Tale of Three Kings* (Carol Stream, IL: Tyndale House, 1992), 15.

CHAPTER 4

ARMY UPDATE: THE UNFOLDING OF WHAT GOD HAD SPOKEN

IN THE PRECEDING chapters, I shared how the Lord spoke to me in 2015 with a very specific message regarding our country and events that were transpiring. But, perhaps, even more amazing is watching what God said unfold before my eyes. In fact, I continue to watch it unfold day by day.

In this chapter and the next, I share how the Lord, our Commander in Chief, has continued amplifying His message of a rising end-time army. This additional insight has both encouraged and challenged me, and I believe it will do the same for you.

One foremost change has been the unwelcome addition of the coronavirus. I think we can all agree that it altered our lives permanently, not just here in America but globally. When the coronavirus fear-mongering began and subsequent closures happened left and right, so many people, including me, just wanted everything to return to normal. By now, we collectively realize that simply won't happen.

However, what has become crystal clear are several things the Lord spoke to me on February 6, 2020. At the time, His words didn't make a lot of sense to me. It was a Thursday morning; I was at my home office just finishing up some notes to come in and speak to my staff, not feeling spiritual at all, and, suddenly, the Lord gave me five individual words. But now I see and understand, and I believe that you will too. We have crossed a line—a point of no return—and we are now accelerating toward the culmination and consummation of the Church age.

Army Composition

If I were to summarize what the Lord revealed to me in His original message in 2015 leading up to this book, *Army of God Rising*, it would be the three following thoughts:

- The Lord said He was assembling His army.
- The Lord said I would be shocked to know who is in this army and who is not. I knew this meant there would be many "frontline" ministers and individuals we would expect to lead this great army but who would be nowhere to be found. There would be others rising up in great leadership capacity, and

we would be asking, "Who is that person?" People who were previously unknowns or the most unlikely would rise to the forefront.

- The Lord said I would be shocked at who I would be joined up with in this army. He said I would connect with people I normally would not connect with or would never expect to emerge as great warriors in the end-time battle.

Since this original book was published in 2016, I have seen all three things unfold in an amazing way—and continue to see it almost daily. People I never expected have become seriously engaged in the various battles at hand. The pastors, ministers, and believers who I thought surely would be leading the way have faded into the distance, many of them disqualified from ministry altogether.

I think we can all agree that the coronavirus debacle became somewhat of a demarcation for everyone. It has changed life for every single one of us no matter where we live.

In March of 2020, Americans were asked to cooperate with our government for a couple of weeks in order to "flatten the curve." We were told that if we didn't, millions of people would die. So, we did just that. It was unprecedented. Businesses were closed, air travel was suspended, churches were shut down except for those that broadcasted their services online, schools closed, and the list goes on and on. We agreed it was our duty and wanted to do our part to prevent millions and millions of people from dying, but nothing even close to what was predicted and projected happened. So, without getting into the weeds of all the hype that was put on the American people and the world, I will attempt to stay on track with the message the Lord delivered to me for this book.

Four Significant Dates

There were significant dates in 2020 that I would like to share with you that I believe pertain to the message of *Army of God Rising*. In hindsight, these dates also have become demarcations for me. Bottom line, we in the Body of Christ have been put on a trajectory, and there is no turning around or slowing down now. If you have ever been serious and committed in your walk with God, it needs to be now. Rid yourself of distractions and unnecessary weights, and run with perseverance the race the Lord has marked for you.

> Hebrews 12:1 NKJV
> *Therefore we also, since we are surrounded by so great a cloud of witnesses, let us lay aside every weight, and the sin which so easily ensnares us, and let us run with endurance the race that is set before us.*

February 2, 2020

It was Super Bowl Sunday. I got home from church and did something a little out of my ordinary routine. I told

Army Update: The Unfolding of What God Had Spoken

my wife after we ate lunch that I was going to watch the Super Bowl. I am not a football fan at all but will certainly watch a game with family and friends if the occasion presents itself. But on that occasion, I would watch the game all by myself. I went downstairs to our big-screen TV and my favorite chair, getting all ready for a relaxing afternoon.

Before I settled in, I went to my desk, plugged in my computer to recharge it, and began thinking, "I wonder who will win the Super Bowl today?" Without any exaggeration, I reached into my desk drawer, pulled out a yellow sticky note, and grabbed a pen. Knowing nothing at all about either of the teams playing that day, the Kansas City Chiefs and the San Francisco 49ers, I wrote *KC*.

Next, I settled into my favorite leather recliner and started watching the game. About the fourth quarter, I thought, "Well, I guess I missed it. The Chiefs aren't going to win this one." Then, in a totally unexpected turn around, the Chiefs scored 21 points and beat the 49ers 31–20. I discovered later on that it had been 50 years since they had claimed a Super Bowl title. When everyone thought there was no way possible for them to win, everything turned around!

I was just as shocked as everyone else who was watching. Then I received a text from my dear friend Kamal Saleem. Many of you know his testimony as a former Jihadist raised in Lebanon, coming to faith in the Lord many years ago. Below, I will print the text I received from Kamal on February 2, 2020, at 10:25 p.m., right after the confetti fell and the celebrations began.

> The tide is turning. This is what the prophet Bob Jones prophesied that when the Kansas City Chiefs win the Super Bowl, the next great move of God would begin! We are excited to see what God is going to do in this turnaround season.

I have to be honest with you, I didn't have a clue as to what Kamal was talking about. I knew of Bob Jones (no relation to the university), but I had never met him or really followed him. I discovered later that he died on February 14, 2014.

I replied to Kamal saying I didn't know anything about that prophecy, but it sounded interesting. I told him that I had watched the entire Super Bowl that evening, which was very unusual for me. Kamal then replied:

> We will see signs and wonders and be one ourselves. This is a big deal for the Kingdom, the beginning of a turnaround for the Church.
>
> When the Kansas City Chiefs win the Super Bowl, the last great end-time move of God would begin.

To my knowledge there is no actual recording of Jones's word from the Lord. I found out later that Kamal had actually spent time with Bob Jones, who shared this word with Kamal personally. There are several other ministers who have reported Bob Jones sharing the same word with them on numerous occasions.

Following this Super Bowl upset, a great deal of information came forth about the significance of the win. Here are some of the more pertinent facts:

- This was the first Super Bowl win for the Chiefs in 50 years that broke their losing streak; 50 is the number of Pentecost and jubilee.
- It was Coach Andy Reid's 222 career win on 2/2/2020.
- The team had a double-digit comeback that set NFL records.
- Interestingly, Bob Jones died on 2/14/2014 and was buried on 2/22/2014.
- The cover of Sports Illustrated reporting on Super Bowl LIV said in big letters "Kingdom Comeback: 50 Years Later…the Chiefs Rule Again."

This is the first of four significant dates that I want to share with you. I didn't think a whole lot about this Super Bowl win and the word that Bob Jones had given until the next significant date, just four days later.

February 6, 2020

It was a Thursday morning, and I was on the calendar to share with our staff at Church For All Nations (CFAN). Staff from both of our campuses come together, and we usually have breakfast together and celebrate personal milestones. It is a really powerful time. Our oldest son,

David, and our daughter-in-law, Hannah, lead the staff in an incredible way. They have developed the absolute best culture we have ever had, and I am blessed to be able to speak to all of them once a month.

Five Important Words

Usually, I pray about what to share before joining the breakfast, but that morning as I packed my briefcase at our home, suddenly the Lord gave me five specific words. In some ways, this was the most unusual way that the Lord has ever spoken to me.

Most of the time, the Lord downloads revelation to me when I am studying the Word, and I will get powerful insights and understanding that come along with it. Anyone who receives revelation of the Word of God or experiences the revelation gifts of the Spirit knows that you can receive something by the Spirit in a moment of time and literally speak or write for hours as to what the Lord has revealed. It was not so that morning. That experience was the most unique encounter I had ever received from the Lord. He simply gave me these five words:

1. Change
2. Upheaval
3. Shifting
4. Redirecting
5. Increase

I quickly wrote down the words on a sticky note. I felt so strongly they were from the Lord, but I had absolutely no insight or revelation about them.

I finished packing up my briefcase and went on to the staff meeting to share what was on my heart for them that day. I also shared the five words with my staff and told them that I had just gotten them from the Lord but had no further revelation. I asked them to pray about the five words and see if the Lord would give them anything. I noticed that some of my staff who are more prophetic were nodding their heads in agreement as I read the words.

The following Sunday, I shared briefly with the congregation that I had received these five words on February 6, but I underscored the fact that I had no further revelation about their meaning. I asked the congregation to pray about them as well.

I remember trying to recall if I had been reading leadership material or had heard someone speak on subjects that could have been related to these words. I thought maybe something I had been studying prompted these words and brought them to the surface in my thinking, but I could not trace them back to anything. Then on Sunday March 15, 2020, these five words began to take on very significant meaning.

Sunday, March 15, 2020

The drive to church that morning for our Sunday services was surreal. The streets of Colorado Springs, Colorado, were empty; it seemed like a ghost town. The church parking lots I passed on the way to our church were empty, and the only cars at CFAN when I arrived were those of the worship team, the media team, and some of the staff.

Because we had been live-streaming our services for years, it was not a particularly huge adjustment other than setting up interactive chat rooms for our congregation watching online. We had also set up a broadcast studio at our home in case there was a complete shutdown.

All these changes combined created major adjustments and a lot of work for all of us, and our staff rose to new levels. They worked harder than ever, and we were so proud of them. Our children's ministry has its own incredible media department and produced separate programming for our kids so they could continue to connect as they had when they were in services on campus.

But an interesting thing happened when I pulled into the church that day, I recalled the statistics that the well-known research firm, The Barna Group, had released. They revealed how churches in America measure success. Barna surveyed 384,000 churches, and the 5 metrics[1] most commonly used to determine success were:

1. Attendance
2. Budget
3. Building square footage in use
4. Number of staff
5. Number of programs offered

Army Update: The Unfolding of What God Had Spoken

So when I pulled into church that morning, I was greeted by an empty parking lot. Walking into the building on my way to an auditorium of empty chairs, I realized that the "metrics for success" many American churches use went completely out the window.

I'm not saying the measurement criteria above are not important, but they really do not have anything to do with making disciples. In all honesty, if these are the metrics we use to determine if we are successful, we are in serious trouble.

Barna also discovered that in the past 2 decades in America, there has been a significant increase of megachurches,[2] but at the same time, professing Christians decreased from 85 percent to 63 percent.[3]

These statistics beg new questions and seriously challenge what we call "success" in Christendom. America enjoys the most religious freedom of any nation (although radically under assault and rapidly disappearing), the greatest prosperity, immense resources, the latest and greatest technology, facilities, and the broadest access to education. So how is it that we are losing our nation?

What do I mean by that? Just one area that strikes at the core of how our nation was founded is the LGBTQ movement. They are less than 3% of the population, and yet they are discipling our schoolchildren in immorality.

In his farewell address in 1796, President George Washington emphasized the importance of preserving freedom of religion within a society:

Of all the dispositions and habits, which lead to political prosperity, Religion and Morality are indispensable supports. In vain would that man claim the tribute of Patriotism, who should labor to subvert these great pillars of human happiness, these firmest props of the duties of Men and Citizens.[4]

We have seen our educational system indoctrinating our children with perversion and godless socialist and Marxist ideologies. We have replaced prayer and Bible reading in our public schools with the most wicked and evil teachings from the very pit of hell, unthinkable just decades ago.

I have been very vocal about these kinds of things and have gained somewhat of a reputation for being "too political" in my preaching. So many have left our church, claiming they want to go "where the Word is preached" and the pastor is more "Christlike." Last time I checked, the Word of God has a great deal to say about life, death, morality, sexuality, and how we live our lives in the public arena. In my opinion, the most un-Christlike behavior occurring in our country today is when ministers are silent about such matters. Our country is starting to realize on a daily basis that these are the things that genuinely matter.

Our lives begin to end the day we become silent about things that matter.

—Martin Luther King, Jr.

So how have we as Americans, in particular the Body of Christ—born into the freest, most prosperous, and most powerful nation in the history of the world—become so weak and impotent? How is it that we have become so marginalized that our very existence as Christians is nearing extinction? It is my conviction that we no longer allow the Lord to build His Church; we have taken over that job and come up with new metrics of what we call success.

We follow Jesus today like we follow someone on Facebook. We "like" Him, though we may never see anything else He has to say or hear from Him again.

I believe that we have created our own version of faith in America that bears little to no resemblance to genuine Bible faith. One great man of God who has influenced my life immensely says, "Faith is not the teaching of the Bible; it is the obeying of the Bible."

In the Old Testament, the king of Egypt broke into the temple of God or the church, so to speak, and took away the shields of gold, which is a type and shadow of faith. In their place, he put shields of brass, which is an alloy. This speaks to what has happened in our American churches; we have a little bit of God and a whole lot of us. It is interesting that in the Scripture, brass speaks of judgment:

> 1 Kings 14:25-27 ASV
>
> *And it came to pass in the fifth year of king Rehoboam, that Shishak king of Egypt came up against Jerusalem; and he took away the treasures of the house of Jehovah, and the treasures*

> *of the king's house; he even took away all: and he took away all the shields of gold which Solomon had made. And king Rehoboam made in their stead shields of brass.*

Yet when we read in our Bibles and see the birth of the New Testament Church in Acts 2, we recognize they had the real thing. Their faith not only allowed them to survive but also to thrive. They destroyed the gates of hell! They transformed the most hostile social and political environments without buildings, religious freedom, professional staff, Twitter, Facebook, or Christian television. John G. Lake describes the early Christians this way:

> In those early centuries of Christianity, Christians did not go into the world apologizing. They went to slay the powers of darkness and undo the works of the devil, and they lived in holy triumph.[5]

This is where God is taking the Church today. Will you join His ranks? There is an *Army of God Rising* at this very moment, and the call is going out for you to join Him! The Lord has put out the call to wake up the mighty men and women of God. It is time to beat your plow into a sword and enter the battle. It is time to seek the Lord as you never have before and repair the broken-down altars of the Lord in your life. It is time to understand that you have everything you need at this very moment; all the authority and all the power you ever will need is *already* inside of you at this very moment in Christ.

So where have we gone wrong in America? Consider these questions and statements that will challenge you and possibly even anger you.

- We have gone from making disciples to merely evangelizing and in the process seeing faulty conversions.
- We have gone from preaching the gospel of the Kingdom to preaching salvation and the new birth, saying little to nothing about the cost of discipleship and following the Lord.
- Have we become peacekeepers instead of being peacemakers? Leonard Ravenhill said, "Preachers who should be fishing for men are now too often fishing for compliments from men."[6]
- Churches have become adult day care centers, designing programs that will fill seats and keep the sheep happy rather than equipping the Body for works of service.
- Are we glorified playgrounds? Do we realize we are in the midst of an intense battle for the eternal souls of men and women? We could be likened to a luxury ship coddling its people, clueless that we need to become a battleship.

The Lord made it clear that those who are born again are the salt of the earth and the light of the world. But when the salt has lost its savor, its ability to disinfect and preserve is nonexistent. This manifests as rottenness and corruption, and all the ills and evils we see in our society right now are here by permission of the Church. Jesus said if we lose our saltiness, we are *"...good for nothing, but to be cast out, and to be trodden under foot of men"* (Matthew 5:13). Based upon the fruit we see in America today, that is where the Church in America stands today.

The Lord also made it clear that we are the light of the world, and when light shines, it always wins in the contest against darkness. So when we compare the early Church to the Church we see in America today, we have a great disparity, which begs the question *why?* We have the same Holy Spirit, the exact same power available to us, and the same faith that was once delivered to the Church. But instead of taking ground, we have lost the ground gained by our founding fathers. *Again, why?* The answer is simple. We have traded in our faith for a form of godliness that denies the power.

> Jude 1:3
>
> *Beloved, when I gave all diligence to write unto you of the common salvation, it was needful for me to write unto you, and exhort you that ye should earnestly contend for the faith which was once delivered unto the saints.*

If there is one thing the coronavirus debacle did for us, it showed us how little power we walk in as the Body of Christ. We sing great songs about no longer being slaves to fear, but then a virus comes along, and everyone begins shaking in their boots. Then, the division that it causes is unprecedented. Church members who had been with us for many years got mad because we did not have services for 11 weeks. Other members got mad because we closed at all, still others got mad because I did not "obey the governor" once we decided to open the church back up for services, and the list goes on and on. I have never seen such division in the Body of Christ. It is entirely okay if we disagree with each other, but let's not become disagreeable with one another.

Now, as I look back, I recognize that the Lord was working in a powerful way. The division in the Body of Christ was accomplishing powerful things. Yes, the devil got some mileage out of it, but the Lord was working His plan. I never thought I would be saying this, but I wouldn't trade this trying time for anything in the world. Paul dealt with this same thing in the Corinthian church.

> 1 Corinthians 11:19 NLT
>
> *But, of course, there must be divisions among you so that you who have God's approval will be recognized.*

Divisions are necessary in the Body of Christ, according to the apostle Paul. As the coronavirus debacle unfolded, I witnessed the Lord working in a tremendous way, and then I understood the reason He gave me those five words on February 6, 2020. He was letting me know that He was with us and bringing about a much bigger plan—*His plan.*

First, He revealed that the Body of Christ was and is not doing as well as we thought we were in America, somewhat like the lukewarm church in Laodicea.

> Revelation 3:15-19 NKJV
>
> *I know your works, that you are neither cold nor hot. I could wish you were cold or hot. So then, because you are lukewarm, and neither cold nor hot, I will vomit you out of My mouth. Because you say, "I am rich, have become wealthy, and have need of nothing"—and do not know that you are wretched, miserable, poor, blind, and naked—I counsel you to buy from Me gold refined in the fire, that you may be rich; and white garments, that you may be clothed, that the shame of your nakedness may not be revealed; and anoint your eyes with eye salve, that you may see. As many as I love, I rebuke and chasten. Therefore be zealous and repent.*

The Lord told the Laodicean church that they were in a pretty sick and pathetic state, and it is because He loves us that He is revealing the same message to us.

We seem to have forgotten the message about discipline, denying ourselves, and the chastening of the Lord. The time for us to be genuinely concerned in our Christian walk is not when we are being chastised by the Lord but when He ceases to correct us.

Hebrews 12:3–8 NKJV

For consider Him who endured such hostility from sinners against Himself, lest you become weary and discouraged in your souls. You have not yet resisted to bloodshed, striving against sin. And you have forgotten the exhortation which speaks to you as to sons: "My son, do not despise the chastening of the Lord, nor be discouraged when you are rebuked by Him; for whom the Lord loves He chastens, and scourges every son whom He receives." If you endure chastening, God deals with you as with sons; for what son is there whom a father does not chasten? But if you are without chastening, of which all have become partakers, then you are illegitimate and not sons.

I do not believe for a minute that the Lord was behind the coronavirus, but He certainly has used it for our benefit. He made it clear to me that three things were happening during this event:

- Sifting: This must occur before there can be a shifting.
- Refining: The Scriptures speak of refining, which is dealing with our faith, moving us from the counterfeit to the genuine (see Malachi 3:1–3; 1 Peter 1:6–7).
- Separating: The wheat must be separated from the chaff, and sheep must be separated

from the goats. Even some of the sheep must be separated from the sheep.

My takeaway during this pandemic is that God has been dealing with His bride, the Body of Christ. It has been a time of revealing and uncovering who we really are and what we have become.

The first three chapters of Revelation have a critical message for the Body of Christ today. They reveal the real Jesus. We live in a time when I hear preachers say, "We need to be more like Jesus!" I couldn't agree more. However, my first question is which Jesus are they referring to—the religious Jesus, the universal Jesus, or the real Jesus?

The religious Jesus is the one who I define as an impostor who dresses up in religious garb and will choke the eternal life out of a person. Those who have grown up with this Jesus will want absolutely nothing to do with God. In many cases, the religious Jesus will churn out atheists in droves and create an immunity to the gospel.

Then there is the universal Jesus who is a sissified, domesticated, effeminate Jesus who avoids controversy at all costs. He is the one who doesn't want to offend anyone and wants to bring us all together in unity at any cost. The universal Jesus uses the Word of God only when it fits the narrative at hand and refuses to weigh in on any type of controversy or make waves.

Then there is the *real* Jesus who is the Way, the Truth, and the Life. He is the One who loved people so much that He revealed the truth to them, so they had the opportunity to accept or reject it for themselves. The real Jesus told us in His own words that He did not come to bring peace but rather division (Luke 12:51), and He would actually set people against one another. He confronted the scribes and Pharisees and their hypocritical ways, calling them out in public and refusing to drink their political Kool-Aid, knowing that it would cost Him His life. This same very real Jesus made a whip and went through the temple flipping tables over and driving out money changers and all those who were merchandising the ministry for selfish gain. I couldn't agree more that we all need to be more like the real Jesus.

May 31, 2020

We opened our church back up on this date, which is the final date that was significant for us at CFAN. We cooperated during the initial coronavirus reports and were sincere in our attempt to be responsible, good neighbors and to make sure that we didn't do anything to bring harm to anyone. But something told us it was enough. Other churches across the nation were doing the same thing; we were not doing it because of anyone else, but we recognized that the Word tells us to not forsake the assembling of ourselves together.

> Hebrews 10:24–25 NKJV
>
> *And let us consider one another in order to stir up love and good works, not forsaking the assembling of ourselves together, as is the manner of some, but exhorting one another, and so much the more as you see the Day approaching.*

It just so happens that May 31, 2020, was Pentecost Sunday, and several other churches had decided to open back up as well. I am not trying to imply that there was something supernatural regarding this particular date; I just think it is interesting that we returned on Pentecost Sunday.

The fact of the matter is that our government lied to us in so many ways. Government overreach went to unprecedented levels, laws that protect citizens were violated, our constitutional rights were violated, and really wicked people were given preferential treatment while the Church and Christians were trampled on. I really hesitate to bring up some of this information because I don't want to detract from the message of what the Lord is saying or doing right now. At the same time, I feel that these are pertinent points.

First and foremost, the citizens of the United States are not stupid. The people get it; they see what is really going on. We have politicians drunk on power, big tech that is subservient to the almighty dollar, and what I call the lame-stream media that are all in bed together and have sold themselves to the highest bidder. They are all tied into the same spirit under the control of the god of this world. There is no way they could possibly coordinate themselves other than through supernatural powers of darkness.

The divisions we have seen both inside and outside of the Church have continued to reveal who has the approval of God upon them and who does not. For instance, when President Donald Trump was in office, I was shocked to see the upheaval that was generated. Whether you like him, love him, or hate him, history will reveal he was the greatest friend to the Church we have had in a president in decades. He fought for religious freedom, yet it seemed that all we heard from so many of the conservatives and the church world was about his past and how mean his tweets were. All the while, the left continued to lie, cheat and steal, and murder the America we love.

The bottom line is that we are in a spiritual war and a cultural revolution in America, with most people being completely unaware of it. Because we do not have blood flowing in the streets, people cannot see it, but we have certainly seen the first fruits of it. I think you get the point that we have lost our way as a nation. I use the analogy that we are suffering from national Alzheimer's—we can no longer recall who we are, where we came from, and where we are headed. We have fallen into self-destructive behavior, and so many things that made America great are being destroyed. We are like an Alzheimer's patient reaching the final stages of the disease when the organs begin to shut down, and death is imminent and in view.

But God!

So back to those five words the Lord gave me. The most incredible things happened during the worst times in recent memory of our nation. Those five words came to pass, and they are even still coming to pass as I write this message.

We saw undeniable *change* that's here to stay. We saw *upheaval* in our ministry, congregation, nation, and world. We had to *shift* so many things and *redirect* resources and our focus, but as we closed 2020 and 2021, we saw unprecedented *increase* in the midst of division and chaos.

In the first four months of 2020, we saw double the number of salvations online compared to the entire previous year of 2019. On one Sunday morning, I thought the counter on the screen was broken when it hit 158 salvations. These are the very definition of a truly good report!

Previously, at the beginning of the "pandemic," we saw many members leave CFAN for various reasons, but we grew and added so many others including faithful members from so many different churches that had decided to remain closed and silent. Our tithes and offerings increased, and we gave a record amount to missions. It was an amount that we had never before been able to give in my 34 years as senior pastor. We also had several people in our church pay their homes off, businessmen and women saw their businesses break records in sales and income, and as a church we eliminated $9.5 million of debt. All of this happened during a challenging time in our nation. We saw the increase the Lord spoke of, and we continue to see it!

It is my sense that the word given about the great move of God that would begin when the Kansas City Chiefs won the Super Bowl was very prophetic in nature. I will never forget thinking to myself that they had lost the game and that I had missed it in thinking they would win. Then came a suddenly—a sudden, miraculous moment!

When it looked like it was over, there was an unlikely and sudden turnaround. Just as *Sports Illustrated* issued a special Super Bowl commemorative edition with the bold headline: "Kingdom Comeback," I believe we are most definitely in the midst of a Kingdom of God comeback.

It is my prayer that you are making yourself ready!

God is assembling His great end-time army to gather in the great final harvest. It is time to reclaim the ground that the devil has stolen. God is calling ordinary people into extraordinary victories. He may not always move quickly, but He does move suddenly, and I pray that you will be ready.

Start breaking up the fallow ground in your life, and seek the Lord as you never have before. He is getting ready to rain down righteousness upon His people, and the harvest will be glorious!

> Hosea 10:12 NKJV
>
> *Sow for yourselves righteousness; reap in mercy; break up your fallow ground, for it is time to seek the Lord, till He comes and rains righteousness on you.*

Notes

1. https://www.charismanews.com/opinion/in-the-line-of-fire/45141-smashing-the-myth-of-american-church-success.

2. There are 1,750 megachurches in the US as of 2020 (http://hartfordinstitute.org/megachurch/2020_Megachurch_Report.pdf) vs 1,611 in the US in 2015 (http://hartfordinstitute.org/megachurch/New-Decade

-of-Megachurches-2011Profile.pdf) vs 1,210 in the US in 2005 (http://hartfordinstitute.org/megachurch/megastoday2005summaryreport.pdf).

3. Self-identified Christians made up 63% of U.S. population in 2021, down from 75% a decade ago (https://www.pewforum.org/2021/12/14/about-three-in-ten-u-s-adults-are-now-religiously-unaffiliated/) vs 85% in 2000 (https://news.gallup.com/poll/2974/america-remains-predominantly-christian.aspx).

4. "George Washington: Farewell Address (1796)," U.S. Embassy & Consulate in South Korea, accessed December 5, 2021, https://kr.usembassy.gov/education-culture/infopedia-usa/living-documents-american-history-democracy/george-washington-farewell-address-1796/#:~:text=Of%20all%20the%20dispositions%20and,duties%20of%20Men%20and%20Citizens.

5. John G. Lake, *Your Power in the Holy Spirit*, comp. Roberts Liardon (New Kensington, PA: Whitaker House, 2010).

6. Leonard Ravenhill, *Why Revival Tarries* (Bloomington, MN: Bethany House Publishers, 1987).

CHAPTER 5

FINISHING WELL

ON THE WAY to church to minister one evening, I had the great privilege of visiting with world-renowned, 20th-century evangelist Dr. Lester Sumrall. The fiery preacher served God like few others, and I always enjoyed benefiting from his great wisdom. That night in the car, he shared a thought that has become invaluable to me.

In my own words, he shared with me that night that life has three semesters: 30 years, 60 years, and 90 years. He explained that years 0 to 30 are your gathering years; you are taking in all life offers. Years 30 to 60 are your production and building years. This is when you are working out all that you have taken in. After 60 years and beyond is when you give back what you have learned from everything you have journeyed through in life. These latter years are your depositing years. And, it is my opinion, that if you will be obedient to the Lord in this particular season of your life, you will do more and accomplish more than in the previous 60 years combined.

In the Hebrew language, there is no word for *retirement*. That makes all the sense in the world to me because, *"The path of the just is as a shining light, that shineth more and more unto the perfect day"* (Proverbs 4:18). The statistics for a person's longevity within a year after truly retiring are alarming. I know of many situations through friends and acquaintances where people have died within a year of their "retirement." Yet God's plan is for the latter years to be the most productive and fruitful season of a person's entire life.

Yes, there are different seasons in our lives, and the workload and specific duties change with each one. Nevertheless, every one of us needs to know God's purpose and plan for our lives every day of our lives. Everyone needs a reason to get up in the morning. My secret to continuous energy is being connected to God's purpose, plan, and vision for me. Every single day I am running with the heavenly vision God has for my life, and you can do the very same thing—even if you have squandered the previous years of your life.

If you still have breath in your lungs, you have purpose!

There are always things to accomplish for the Kingdom of God! He has the power to restore *all* that the enemy has stolen from your life (see Joel 2:18-27).

The purpose and message of this book is to share with you that God is assembling His army at this very moment, and He has a place in it for *you!*

You may not feel qualified or think you have anything to offer. You may not believe you are even worthy to be a part of it, but that kind of thinking is completely irrelevant. What you may not know is God has the supernatural ability to take everything in your life—the good, the bad, the ugly—and make it into something beautiful and powerful that will make a difference for eternity, even if you are at the very end of your life!

Oftentimes, it is out of the *mess* that we have made in our lives that the really powerful "mess-age" that God wants to deliver through us comes forth.

Peter Daniels, a wealthy entrepreneur with an incredible life story, shared something with me in a very similar vein. I first met him in 1998 when he came to speak at our church. At that time of his life, he had read over 5,000 biographies and autobiographies of both Christian and non-Christian leaders. He shared with me that his observation after extensive reading was this: people spend their whole lives getting ready for what they are really destined to do. It is true in the lives of businesspeople, military leaders, politicians, ministers, and the list could go on.

I heard someone challenge an audience once by saying, "Don't be a generational thief! Don't take what took you a lifetime to learn to the grave with you." That stayed with me! Think of the lessons you have learned throughout your life and the price you had to pay to learn them. I can promise you that there is someone, somewhere, going through exactly what you have already been through; and your wisdom, encouragement, and input could help them get through it. In fact, your wisdom from experience may even save their lives.

We should write about our experiences and talk about them. We should preach, teach, and pour into those who are hungry to learn the benefits of our experience and the wisdom it taught us. Make it so others can start where you leave off instead of starting where you began. <u>In life, the more you give away, the more you receive back</u>.

This is what I have attempted to do in this book. I have shared with you what I have discovered in my walk with the Lord. These are things I have heard directly from Him and some of what I have learned and discerned that is necessary to help you finish well in life.

This quote makes my point: "I don't like to pay for the same real estate twice." It is my prayer that the Body of Christ quits *paying for the same real estate over and over*. As the Lord is now assembling His great end-time army, I pray that you will find supernatural strength and synergism as you find your God-ordained place in Him.

The concept of finishing well is an entirely Christian concept, and the Scriptures speak specifically about it. The world has the most convoluted idea of what it is to *finish well* that is summed up in the statement, "He who dies with the most toys wins." That may sound good to some people, but they might want to add: "But he is still dead." It is what comes after death that people need to pay attention to. The bottom line is this: you will *not* finish well— no matter how much you achieve and succeed in life—unless you receive the Lord and come into a divine alignment with Him.

Not all success in this life is good success. There have been millions of people who have "succeeded," yet they are in hell at this very moment. God gave us the master key to *"good success"* in Joshua 1, which we will read yet again.

> Joshua 1:8 NKJV
>
> *This Book of the Law shall not depart from your mouth, but you shall meditate in it day and night, that you may observe to do according to all that is written in it. For then you will make your way prosperous, and then you will have good success.*

God's law is His Word. It is His instruction, and you can't get any better instruction than that. The counsel of the Lord is immutable, meaning that it is the absolute highest truth; therefore, it is unchangeable because God is all-knowing, all-wise, and all-powerful.

The Lord makes it clear to Joshua, and anyone who wants good success, that you must fully embrace the Word of God in thought, word, and deed. This means you have to change your vocabulary and start speaking life: *"Death and life are in the power of the tongue"* (Proverbs 18:21). Then when His Word becomes the meditation of your heart and you do what it says you should do, you will make your way prosperous and have good success.

Solomon, the richest and wisest man who has ever lived in the history of the world, had some advice for people who have a temporal view of success.

Ecclesiastes 2:4-11 NLT

I also tried to find meaning by building huge homes for myself and by planting beautiful vineyards. I made gardens and parks, filling them with all kinds of fruit trees. I built reservoirs to collect the water to irrigate my many flourishing groves. I bought slaves, both men and women, and others were born into my household. I also owned large herds and flocks, more than any of the kings who had lived in Jerusalem before me. I collected great sums of silver and gold, the treasure of many kings and provinces. I hired wonderful singers, both men and women, and had many beautiful concubines. I had everything a man could desire!

So I became greater than all who had lived in Jerusalem before me, and my wisdom never failed me. Anything I wanted, I would take. I denied myself no pleasure. I even found great pleasure in hard work, a reward for all my labors. But as I looked at everything I had worked so hard to accomplish, it was all so meaningless—like chasing the wind. There was nothing really worthwhile anywhere.

Solomon actually became a conduit of the wisdom of God. Proverbs is a profound book that has imparted wisdom to me that has not only changed my life in profound ways, but has also in some cases even saved it. Yet, with all of the profound wisdom flowing through Solomon, he did not have a good ending; he did not finish well.

Recently, I was with a pastor friend having a discussion about the concept of finishing well. In the Bible there are somewhere around 3,000 people mentioned, and only 100 finished. And of the 100 that finished, only 30 finished well. The more shocking part is: of the remaining 70, about half of them flamed out at the very end.

The question is: How will you finish for the Lord?

Your Margin of Victory

I have a little motivational book in my library titled *212* that comes with a four-minute DVD. It is an inspiring little book that reveals the power of effort, perseverance, and focus. Its message will encourage and inspire each of us to finish well.

For example, water is hot at 211 degrees Fahrenheit, but it will boil at 212 degrees. An increase of just one degree can transform hot water and make it boiling water. Little things make a huge difference. Small keys open big doors. The hinges that the door of faith swings on are generally never noticed, but important nonetheless.

The average margin of victory in professional golf for over 25 years was less than 3 strokes. The average margin of victory between an Olympic gold medal and no medal in 2004 for the men's 800-meter race was .71 seconds. The average margin of victory for the Indy 500 over a 10-year period was 1.54 seconds.

The edge that exists between victory and defeat is a very thin line. I want to point out that small things may not seem that important, but in fact, small things may be the margin of victory that you need in your life. There are "little things" that you can do as an individual, family, church community, state, and even as a nation that can bring radical change. Ask the Lord even now what small changes and adjustments you need to make in order to gain great victories for this *Army of God Rising*.

Let me offer three simple things you can do to join the ranks of this *Army of God Rising*. In fact, these steps are so easy they may seem anticlimactic, but they come directly from the Lord Himself and are found in Matthew 7. Simply put: ask, seek, and knock.

Matthew 7:7 says, *"Ask, and it will be given to you; seek, and you will find; knock, and it will be opened to you. For everyone who asks receives, and he who seeks finds, and to him who knocks it will be opened"* (NKJV).

If you read this scripture in the Amplified Bible, Classic Edition, it says to ask and keep on asking, to seek and keep on seeking, and to knock and keep on knocking. This is the indication of a person who is spiritually hungry, someone who cannot and will not be denied. Those who are spiritually hungry will be blessed to an overflowing measure.

James 1:5 promises us that if we lack wisdom, we merely need to ask the Lord, and He will give it to us. The Commander of God's Army is faithful to keep His Word!

I pray that you will enlist today in the *Army of God Rising*. Jesus said that the harvest is plentiful, but the laborers are few; and there has never been a greater time to be alive than this very moment. I pray the passion of our God has been ignited within you to engage the society around you and see our culture shift back to all that made our nation great!

CHAPTER 6

LOOKING FORWARD WITH EXPECTATION

WHEN WE LOOK back in history at the great moves of God, the focus was most often upon the preachers who led those revivals and were at the forefront of those outpourings. Yet I have sensed for years that this last great outpouring of the Holy Spirit that is upon us even now will be radically different, and I want to conclude by looking forward with expectancy for what's been spoken about the end-time *Army of God Rising*.

As I was completing my final edits and reviews of this book, I made a quick trip to Tulsa, Oklahoma, with my oldest son, David. While I was driving into the office on the morning of our departure, I decided to text a minister friend of mine, Tony Cooke, to see if he had dinner plans for that evening. He responded back saying he and his wife already had plans to go out to dinner, but we were welcome to join them.

We were enjoying a great time of fellowship when George Washington Carver came up in our conversation. Tony asked me if I recalled the prediction that Carver made regarding the last end-time move of God. He pointed out that Carver said,

> There is going to be a great spiritual awakening in the world, and it is going to come from... plain, simple people who know—not simply believe—but actually know that God answers prayer. It is going to be a great revival of Christianity, not a revival of religion. This is going to be a revival of true Christianity.... It is going to rise from the laymen, from men who are going about their work and putting God into what they do, from men who believe in prayer and who want to make God real to mankind.[1]

As we continued talking, I realized that I was suddenly getting the closing words for this book you are now reading. Tony continued to share additional quotes by other great men of God that confirmed what has been stirring in my heart about the end times that we are in even now.

Another quote Tony shared was from Charles S. Price who wrote the book *The Real Faith* published in 1940. Price was originally from Britain and trained in law at Wesley College, Oxford. He had a conversion experience at a Free Methodist Mission in Spokane, Washington, under the ministry of Aimee Semple McPherson, when he went to her meeting to gather material to expose her. The plan to expose her backfired, and, at a later meeting, he was filled with the Holy Spirit and spoke in other tongues, which was something he was determined not to do. From that time on, he became a blazing flame of evangelism and a channel for divine healing wherever he went. Often more than 10,000 people attended his meetings.[2] Charles Price once said concerning the last-day outpouring of the Holy Spirit, "Laymen will be His [God's] most important channel—not the clergy, or the theologians, or the great gifted preachers, but men and women with ordinary jobs in the ordinary world."

Mordecai Hamm, who was the evangelist the Lord used to bring Billy Graham to the Lord in Charlotte, North Carolina, in 1934, said something similar. Hamm said that God had given him a revelation that it would be ordinary men and women of God who would reach the world with the gospel. Hamm called laymen "...the sleeping giant of evangelism."

D.L. Moody, renowned 19th-century American evangelist and publisher, made the statement, "If this world is going to be reached, I am convinced that it must be done by men and women of average talent."

To me the Great Commission is the greatest mission, vision, strategy, and core value statement ever uttered. It is clear, concise, and perfectly complete in content. Jesus told His disciples, "I have been given all authority in Heaven and on earth. *Therefore, go!*"

Notice that Jesus did not say, "Go and hold mass crusades," or "Fill up stadiums," etc., although I love to see all of that and think we should be holding mass crusades. But Jesus said it best when He said, "Make disciples of *all* nations, *all* people." Go near, go far, go to one, or fill stadiums and hold mass crusades with many—but by all means *go!* The Great Commission *cannot* be fulfilled any other way. Some 95 percent of people who come to know the Lord do so through an individual relationship of a family member or friend.

In fact, I have heard it said that if we counted seats in all Christian and Catholic churches and every Jewish synagogue in the world, it is believed that less than 2% of the world's population could fit into them. Face the facts! We will never get all the world into church buildings—even if they were inclined to come. Therefore, the Church—the Body of Christ—must *go into all the world!*

For the sake of illustration, let's say that we wanted to visit and reach every single person on planet Earth with the gospel either for the very first time or one last time. Of the 7 billion-plus people alive today, if we could win 1,000 of them to the Lord every single day (365 days a year), it would take in excess of 19,000 years to reach them. So, we are back to what Jesus commanded us to do from the very beginning—to go make disciples who can go make disciples who can go make even more disciples. Then, we can reach the world in a relatively short amount of time!

Tommy Hicks was a major figure in the powerful 1954 Argentina Revival, who had a stunning vision of the end-time move of God. I encourage you to find it and read it! He made the following statement that I believe sums up who will be in this great end-time army of God.

"God is going to take the do-nothings, the nobodies, the unheard-of, the no-accounts. He is going to take every man and every woman, and He is going to give to them this outpouring of the Spirit of God."

It has been difficult to get people involved in the things of God in days gone by; however, there is a promise that a day is coming when God's people will be ready and willing to gather in the harvest. *"Thy people shall be willing in the day of thy power"* (Psalm 110:3).

The last great move of God has already started. I believe that so much of what you have gone through in the last several years and even decades will soon begin to make a great deal of sense. There is a mighty *Army of God Rising*, and it is my prayer that you will join the ranks.

NOTES

1. George Washington Carver, *The Man Who Talks with the Flowers,* (Macalester Park Publishing) page 37.
2. Charles S. Price, *The Real Faith*, page iii of the Preface (1940).

About the Author

During my senior year of high school in 1976, the Lord began to strongly draw me to Himself. At the time, I was working in Colorado Springs, Colorado, and He sent a Nazarene Bible college student across my path who had a genuine walk with the Lord. To be honest, he made me absolutely miserable. There was nothing phony about this gentleman at all. The fact is that his very life convicted me of my need to surrender to the Lord. It wasn't so much what he said but who he was. Finally, in 1977, I gave my life completely to the Lord.

Fast-forward to 1983, I started attending the church that I now pastor. It was originally started in July of 1979 as Faith Christian Fellowship (FCF). The umbrella church was started by Buddy Harrison in Tulsa, Oklahoma, in 1978, and if my memory serves me correctly, we were the second FCF church started out of the Tulsa church. Shortly after I began attending, I got to know the senior pastor. He recognized the call of God on my life, and he invited me to be a part-time staff member.

I had always had a heart to serve and thoroughly enjoyed serving, but I never ever thought I would be a senior pastor. As I look back in hindsight, I can see that the Lord had a definite path prepared for me to walk—one I could never have dreamed of. The words of the apostle Paul in Ephesians 2:10 (AMP) resonate strongly in my heart when I think of my start in ministry.

For we are His workmanship [His own master work, a work of art], created in Christ Jesus [reborn from above—spiritually transformed, renewed, ready to be used] for good works, which God prepared [for us] beforehand [taking paths which He set], so that we would walk in them [living the good life which He prearranged and made ready for us].

I believe that God has a plan for every single human being from the moment they come alive in the womb. When we open the doors of our hearts, invite Him in, and make Him Lord of our lives, something supernatural begins to transpire. It is God, Himself, who orders your steps toward His perfect will for your life.

I believe that from conception, God has a book with every day of our lives written and planned out. But we must also remember that we have an adversary, and the war over our lives begins at conception. This is why there are so many abortions in the world; the devil both hates and fears every single human being because each one is a special creation of God.

Whenever I share the gospel, I often tell people, "The Lord has a plan for your life, and it is a very detailed and beautiful plan, one that is beyond comprehension." King David in the Old Testament said it well:

Psalm 139:16 AMP

Your eyes have seen my unformed substance; and in Your book were all written the days that were appointed for me, when as yet there was not one of them [even taking shape].

But you can never forget that our adversary is fully set to steal, kill, and destroy. There are intense spiritual battles that will come against every single person to stop God's plan from happening.

When I answered the call of God upon my life, I had absolutely no idea the challenges and difficulties I would encounter. And, if I had known the half of it, the temptation to do something entirely different with my life would have been strong and appealing.

In 1984, a woman named Linda began attending my church and volunteering her commercial art skills. As it turns out, we ended up working on projects together and recognized the Lord was involved in our meeting each other. We were married on January 21, 1985. That very same month, there was a transition of the founding pastor and a new incoming senior pastor, who then invited Linda and me to be his associate pastors.

At this time, the church had tremendous difficulties and challenges, and, quite honestly, the new pastor had four strikes against him before he ever got started. There was a severely wounded congregation that felt betrayed by the founding pastor, there were excessive debts, the building was in great disrepair, and various scandals had transpired, including a new administrator who ultimately went to prison for his business dealings outside the church. There were also potential lawsuits pending. There were witches and satanists who planted themselves in the congregation, and there was charismatic witchcraft coming from members who thought they knew the direction the church should go. All told, it was a formula for disaster for anyone. The second senior pastor endured all of this for a full two years, and then he felt called to go back to Texas to pastor a church that was waiting for him and his wife.

So in January 1987, Linda and I began our journey as senior pastors, and it was a journey I would have never chosen. I felt so ill-equipped and inept. I argued with the Lord that He made a poor choice in bringing us into the position of senior pastors. I never wanted to have a senior pastor position to begin with; I was always so content to serve and help wherever I could. But early on when I gave my life to the Lord, I committed to do His will—whatever it was and wherever it took me.

So if I could summarize all the years since Linda and I became senior pastors, I would have to say that if it were not for the Lord, we never would have survived. To borrow a quote, "I wouldn't give you a dime to go through what we have been through, but you couldn't give me any amount of money for what I have learned." But, far more valuable than anything I have learned is what I have become. For the most part, until people get to the place in life where they really *need* God, they probably won't ever have any time for Him. At that time of our lives, we absolutely, positively needed God, or we simply weren't going to make it.

Here are a few things that helped me navigate the difficult spots along the way. This is certainly not an exhaustive list, but these continue to serve me well today:

- If you don't get bitter, you can indeed get better.
- If you are always fixing the blame, you will never be able to fix the problem.
- The same sunshine that hardens clay, melts butter. My response to the challenges of life determines the outcome. There came a point when I had to decide that I would not allow my heart to harden toward the Lord. He is not my problem; He is my Deliverer! This challenged me in the area of forgiveness toward those who had wronged me and were praying against me and the church. The Lord let me know, in no uncertain terms, that how I handle offenses would either be my stepping-stone or my tombstone.
- It was not the happenings without that determined my success or failure but the happenings within me. All power for the believer comes from within, and although we we can't control what happens around us, we most certainly control what happens inside of us.

- Praying in tongues is one of the most important weapons and tools that the Lord has put in my arsenal. There have been so many times when I simply did not know how to pray as I ought. Praying with the Spirit is one of the most powerful weapons in our arsenal that not only builds us up spiritually but devastates the enemy.

God has prearranged a plan for you also to walk in the good life we discussed above. Invite Him into your heart and life, and begin walking in the steps He's ordered for you.

OUR VISION

Proclaiming the truth and the power of the Gospel of Jesus Christ with excellence. Challenging Christians to live victoriously, grow spiritually, know God intimately.

Connect with us on
Facebook @ **HarrisonHousePublishers**
and Instagram @ **HarrisonHousePublishing**
so you can stay up to date with news
about our books and our authors.

Visit us at **www.harrisonhouse.com**
for a complete product listing as well as
monthly specials for wholesale distribution.